Working Together for Local Integration of Migrants and Refugees in Berlin

This document, as well as any data and any map included herein, are without prejudice to the status of or sovereignty over any territory, to the delimitation of international frontiers and boundaries and to the name of any territory, city or area.

Please cite this publication as:
OECD (2018), *Working Together for Local Integration of Migrants and Refugees in Berlin*, OECD Publishing, Paris.
https://doi.org/10.1787/9789264305236-en

ISBN 978-92-64-30522-9 (print)
ISBN 978-92-64-30523-6 (PDF)

The statistical data for Israel are supplied by and under the responsibility of the relevant Israeli authorities. The use of such data by the OECD is without prejudice to the status of the Golan Heights, East Jerusalem and Israeli settlements in the West Bank under the terms of international law.

Photo credits:
Cover © Marianne Colombani

Foreword

When it comes to migrant integration, the local level matters. Where migrants go and how they integrate into their new communities depends on the specific characteristics of cities and regions. Even though migration policies are the responsibility of the national government, the concentration of migrants in cities, and particularly in metropolitan areas, has an impact on the local demand for work, housing, goods and services that local authorities have to manage. Local authorities play a vital role in this integration. Cities can learn from each other and help provide local, regional, national and international policy makers and practitioners with better evidence for integration policy design.

This case study Working Together for Local Integration of Migrants and Refugees in Berlin provides insight into Berlin's migrant integration trends and current situation. In order to do so it applies the OECD Checklist for public action on migrant integration at the local level that is articulated around 4 blocks and 12 objectives. The four blocks cover: 1) institutional and financial settings; 2) time and proximity as keys for migrants and host communities to live together; 3) enabling conditions for policy formulation and implementation; and 4) sectoral policies related to integration: access to the labour market, housing, social welfare and health, and education.

This case study is part of a broader OECD-European Union project "A territorial approach to migrant integration: The role of local authorities" which addresses a critical gap in knowledge on migration issues by analysing the multi-level governance of local integration. This project takes stock of such multi-level governance frameworks and policies for migrant and refugee integration at the local level in nine large European cities: Amsterdam, Athens, Barcelona, Berlin, Glasgow, Gothenburg, Paris, Rome and Vienna and, thanks to the support of the German Ministry for Economic Affairs and Energy, a small city in Germany (Altena). It also builds on information collected from these and 61 other European cities (35 of which are in Germany, including Düsseldorf, Munich and the Region of Hannover), through an ad-hoc survey and a newly created and publicly available statistical database on migrant outcomes at regional level. The study looks at updates to the governance mechanisms that cities adopted in the wake of the influx of asylum seekers and refugees that interested EU countries since 2015. Conversely, it also investigates opportunities to extend some of the services recently established for newcomers to long-standing migrant groups.

This and the other nine city case studies, along with the synthesis report Working Together for Local Integration of Migrants and Refugees, are outputs of this OECD-European Union initiative contributing to the programme of work of the OECD Regional Development Policy Committee (RDPC) in the Centre for Entrepreneurship, SMEs, Regions and Cities. They also contribute to the OECD Horizontal Project on "Ensuring the effective integration of vulnerable migrant groups" by focusing on improving the integration capacities of the local governments.

Acknowledgements

This publication Working Together for Local Integration of Migrants and Refugees in Berlin was produced by the Centre for Entrepreneurship, SMEs, Regions and Cities (CFE) led by Lamia Kamal-Chaoui, Director. It is part of a wider project "A territorial approach to migrant integration: The role of local authorities" and an output of an OECD-European Union initiative contributing to the programme of work of the OECD's Regional Development Policy Committee (RDPC).

Co-ordination of the wider project and this case study was led by Claire Charbit, Head of the Territorial Dialogue and Migration Unit in the Regional Development and Tourism Division managed by Alain Dupeyras, in CFE. This case study has been drafted by Viviane Spitzhofer (OECD/CFE and external expert) and Lisanne Raderschall (OECD/CFE), with substantive inputs and contributions from Anna Piccinni (OECD/CFE). This report further benefitted from the participation of Johannes Weber (OECD/STI) and Paola Proietti (OECD/CFE). The team is grateful for the support received from the OECD Berlin Centre, notably Heino von Meyer, Head of the Centre. This case study also benefitted from the comments of colleagues across OECD directorates, in particular Thomas Liebig and Eva Degler from the International Migration Division of the Directorate for Employment, Labour and Social Affairs (ELS).

The case study has been developed thanks to the close collaboration of the Municipality of Berlin that provided the information and organised the OECD field work. The Secretariat would like to express its gratitude to all the participants to the interviews (see Annex A), in particular national government representatives and the staff of the municipality. Special thanks go to Andreas Germershausen, Doris Nahawandi, Kai Leptien, Nele Allenberg, Dr. Tillmann Löhr, Barbara Berninger and Ayten Dogan, for their support throughout the development of the case study.

The Secretariat is especially thankful for the financial contribution and the collaboration throughout the implementation of the project to the European Union Directorate-General for Regional and Urban Policy. In particular, the Secretariat would like to thank Andor Urmos and Louise Bonneau for their guidance as well as for their substantive inputs during the revision of the case study.

Table of contents

Boxes

Tables

Figures

Abbreviations and acronyms

BAMF	Bundesamt für Migration und Flüchtlinge [Federal Office for Migration and Refugees
BMAS	Bundesministerium für Arbeit und Soziales [Federal Ministry for Labour- and Social Affairs]
BMI	Bundesministerium des Inneren, für Bau und Heimat [Federal Ministry of the Interior, Building and Community]
BVV	Bezirksverordnetenversammlung [District Parliament]
EASY	Erstverteilung von Asylbegehrenden [Initial distribution of asylum seekers]
EU	European Union
FIM	Flüchtlingsintegrationsmaßnahmen [Refugee Integration Measures]
IMK	Innenministerkonferenz [Permanent Conference of Ministers and Senators for the Interior of the Federal Länder]
IntMK	Integrationsministerministerkonferenz [Conference of Ministers for Integration of the Länder]
LADS	Landesstelle für Gleichbehandlung - gegen Diskriminierung [State Office for Equal Treatment and Against Discrimination]
LAF	Landesamt für Flüchtlinge [State Office for Refugees]
LAGeSo	Landesamt für Gesundheit und Soziales [Regional Department for Health and Social Affairs]

Executive summary

Berlin has long been known as a multicultural and diverse city. Today, the city is home to roughly 3.5 million people, of which around 30% have a migration background, i.e. they themselves or at least one of their parents were not born with German citizenship. Across Germany, those with a migration background represented 23% of the total population in 2016. While in the 1950s to 1970s migrants mostly came from Turkey, Poland and the Russian Federation, in 2015 almost half (46%) of the migrants who moved to Berlin originated from a European country and of these, 72% originated from an EU member state. Despite having a long political tradition of migrant integration, Berlin struggles to bridge wide socio-economic gaps between people with and without a migration background. For example, there is a 10 percentage point difference between the unemployment rates for people with a migration background than for those without.

The particularly high numbers of asylum seekers in 2015 (33 300) and in 2016 (27 247) fundamentally challenged the city's response capacities. It also highlighted the need for a renewal of administrative procedures linked to the reception and integration of refugees and asylum seekers. This increase also triggered a reflection on the integration delays of long-standing migrant groups. It helped to bring the topic of migrant integration back on the local political agenda, leading to the establishment of new integration measures in addition to the already existing focus on equal participation. It also includes increased reliance on, but also recognition of, civil society engaged in the integration of refugees as well as migrants. Innovative measures and pilot programmes currently being tested for asylum seekers and refugees might also open opportunities that allow for an expansion of target groups if proven successful.

The city's double role as a city and a Land (federal state) is a double-edged sword regarding migrant integration. It increases the city's competences in many policy areas relevant to integration, but also hampers flexibility and timely adjustments to cross-sectoral policy challenges due to its complex administrative governance structure. The city's main policy document, which structures its approaches to migrant integration, is the 2010 Participation and Integration Act (PartIntG). As the first *Länder* integration act in Germany, it signifies an important milestone for Berlin to ensure intercultural openness and equal participation of people with a migration background in the city. It also designates Berlin's Commissioner for Migration and Integration as head of a unit dealing exclusively with issues regarding migration and integration.

The main aim of this case study is to reflect on and analyse how integration and reception of migrants and refugees is organised across different levels of government, what responsibilities the city has and its interaction with other stakeholders. The study is structured according to the 12 objectives identified in the OECD Checklist for public action on migrant integration at the local level, as outlined in the 2018 OECD report Working Together for Local Integration of Migrants and Refugees.

Key Findings

What is already being done and how it could be improved

Vertical Co-ordination

Thanks to its dual status as a city and a *Land*, Berlin often seems to be well integrated into a variety of vertical co-ordination mechanisms that allow for fluid relations between the city and *Land* administration. Like many other *Länder*, it contributed to the development of Germany's National Action Plan for Integration (2012), previously the 2005 National Integration Plan, which aims to coordinate integration policy making across government levels. Berlin takes part in the institutionalised dialogue Conference of Ministers for Integration of the *Länder* (*Integrationsministerministerkonferenz*, IntMK), which was established in 2006 to coordinate the actions of regions. Once a year, the 16 regional ministers responsible for integration affairs come together to discuss recent challenges in the field of integration and migration. In addition to the Conference, the IntMK biannually publishes a state integration monitoring report (*Integrationsmonitioring der Länder*) including an important set of indicators measuring various dimensions of social integration compared across *Länder*. Nevertheless, broader co-ordination mechanisms that span across all levels of government – regularly including also the city level – are rather scarce.

Co-ordination at city level and cross-sectoral policy coherence

Berlin's dual administrative structure as a city-state is complex and involves multiple stakeholders, competencies and projects. In order to prevent units from working in silos, the city makes efforts for more participative management. For instance, in 2016 the Masterplan Integration and Security was a quick policy response to provide a comprehensive framework for reception and integration for refugees starting from Day One. Learning from past experience, the Masterplan includes several measures that re-structure and develop the settlement process, including cooperation measures between federal and *Länder* levels for language training or the installation of an office for employment consultation in refugee accommodation.

This policy framework was expanded in 2018 into the Concept for Integration and Participation of Refugees. The municipality involved all city departments, as well as refugee associations, in a consultative process starting with a conference to collect refugee views and to develop ideas in working groups. Additional good practices in co-ordination are institutional venues such as the Council of Mayors, facilitating exchange among districts, and the Conference of the Integration Commissioners, which takes place at the *Länder* and city level. Yet, concrete co-ordination rounds are mostly initiated on an ad hoc basis in response to recent challenges and could benefit from institutionalisation. The participation of district representatives and the strengthening of their competencies could also be improved. As districts are big, both in geographical size and population, they themselves are diverse and have specific needs, potentials and challenges to address. District representatives and local stakeholders are thus key actors in providing knowledge and oversight of local level needs.

Berlin sets itself apart from other *Länder* as its work on migrant integration is grounded in a legal act: the first regional Participation and Integration Act (PartIntG) in Germany established in 2010. Berlin was followed by North-Rhine-Westphalia (2012), Baden-Wuerttemberg (2015), and Bavaria (2016). The Act provides a framework defining the cross-sectoral tasks and measures for all public entities. It also identifies Berlin's Commissioner for Migration and Integration as a head of a unit exclusively dealing with these issues for the whole city, as well as Commissioners for Migration and Integration at district level.

Evaluation mechanisms

Both the biannual report (*Integrationsmonitioring der Länder*) that Berlin, like all German Länder, contributes to for the IntMK and the report on the implementation of the integration law (PartIntG) published every two years by the *Land* are unique integration evaluation tools that Berlin benefits from in its double role as Land and city. However, the city could improve evaluation by developing clear objectives and benchmarks, in particular in the area of intercultural openness, to clarify this rather abstract notion and enhance enforcement mechanisms to ensure that the results of the evaluation are implemented across public and private bodies.

Strengthening migrant pupil integration in schools

Migrant children with special support needs attend "welcome" classes before they can switch to regular classes at all levels of schooling. Since 2014, the city has developed an optional training course for teachers of welcome classes. Since the increase in welcome classes (from 120 in 2012 to 1 051 in 2017), the schools that establish welcome classes receive general funding for additional teacher positions and expenditures from the Berlin Senate. However, the Senate is trying to update the concept of separate welcome classes that in many schools failed to integrate pupils into regular classes. New concepts have been tested, including a new curricula and a framework guiding schools on integration of newcomers, for instance making intercultural education compulsory for all pupils. The regional co-ordination centres are considered a good co-ordination example by the Senate Department for Education as they run initial testing of newcomers determining individual possibilities to transfer directly to regular classes or vocational placement.

Some remaining challenges and how they are addressed

Educational attainment and integration in the labour market

People in Berlin with a migration background still lag severely behind the native-born population in terms of educational attainment and the employment rate. For instance, unemployment is 10 percentage points higher for people with a migration background than for people without a migration background. The poverty risk in Berlin for people with a migration background is three times higher than for people without. The city has instituted programmes to match young people with a migration background with local labour force needs and to increase educational attainment. For instance "Berlin Needs You!" intervenes at an early stage in schools and links public employers and large private companies and candidates for potential apprenticeships. Currently 30 schools and 60 employers are part of the programme.

Housing, geographical concentration of migrant populations in the city and spaces for interaction

In the last five years, the net-migration balance for Berlin indicated a surplus of approximately 48 700 people per year, and the expected future trend is for further increases. Consequently, affordable housing is and will be increasingly scarce. Statistics indicate that people with a migration background experience worse housing conditions than native Germans. The personal living space for families with children under 18 is, on average, 7.7 m² smaller for people with a migration background than for people without a migration background. Berlin's main approach to improve the housing situation is to increase the social housing stock. Subsidies are also provided to landlords who build new housing projects anywhere in the city. These apartments can only be rented to low-income households with a rent subject to caps.

Socio-economically weaker districts of Berlin often have strong concentrations of foreign-born people and their children. While in some cities studied for this project people with a migration background are largely situated on the outskirts of the city, the share of people with a migration background in Berlin is higher in some areas of the centre of the city than in its suburbs. These are Wedding (part of district Mitte), the north-east district of Friedrichshain-Kreuzberg and in the north of Neukölln. Settlements of people with a migration background in distinct neighbourhoods are in general motivated by cheaper housing prices and availability of social housing as well as the presence of relatives and an incumbent migrant community.

Exchanges could be facilitated by creating more shared public spaces that allow for interaction and encounters between foreign-born and local populations. These could enhance understanding and inclusion of both sides and could possibly ease public support and positive communication. Some initiatives have been implemented through the project "Social City", which is a federal initiative. The initiative is a participatory programme to stabilise and upgrade neighbourhoods that are disadvantaged from a social, economic and urban planning perspective. The approach aims to create social cohesion and foster interaction in areas and neighbourhoods in Berlin. This is done by combining local social festivities with changes in the urban infrastructure, making spaces more attractive to rest, play and exercise by increasing open spaces and vegetation. Participating venues aim in particular to promote intercultural exchanges through inclusion of all groups residing in the area and engage local stakeholders. Each neighbourhood is equipped with an office and a neighbourhood management team that functions as a focal point.

Housing for asylum seekers and beneficiaries of international protection

As of March 2018, about 1 500 asylum seekers were living in temporary emergency accommodation. This is problematic as they offer limited private space and often lack infrastructure (kitchens, bathrooms, etc.) to serve many people. During the peak of arrivals (2015-2016) and the resulting need for quickly available accommodation, operators were tendered in a short-term procedure but lacked quality checks, which caused problems as some operators did not provide adequately-trained staff, or meet basic health standards. In light of the deficits in accommodations, the Senate established a quality-check work group in the State Office for Refugees and adjusted the tendering process to ensure quality. Once protection is granted, beneficiaries of the subsidiary protection status who hold a 12-month residence permit generally find it challenging to move out of collective housing facilities, also because of the limited availability of housing stock. The social housing stock is about to be increased since the city has built the so-called "tempohomes", temporary state-owned lightweight housing. In order to avoid segregation and exclusion, newly-established facilities are spread throughout the city.

Practices that could be replicated

Intercultural capacities of municipal staff

According to its Integration and Participation Act, all of Berlin's institutions must ensure advanced training in intercultural competences for their employees and consider this a relevant skill in recruiting. Developments are monitored and have to be reported back to the legislative political entity, i.e. the city's parliament.

Time and the need to accompany migrants throughout their entire lives

Berlin has learned from past experience and has recently developed a support system for newcomers, asylum seekers, refugees and migrants from moment zero until settling in. Multiple entry points were installed to ensure consistent presence and provide easy access to information about legal aspects, housing, education and work matters as well as everyday life. These include the installation of fixed venues like Welcome Center Berlin or Welcome-to-Work Offices in large refugee accommodations, but also mobile services such as the Berlin mobile education counselling service *(Berliner Bidungsberatung MoBiBe)* as well as the Integration Guides, who individually accompany newly-arrived migrants as well as migrants who have resided in the city for a longer time but still require assistance. The guides act in close cooperation with public services and this close interaction has proven to be a success.

Consultative mechanisms to ensure migrant and refugee participation

A good example for the involvement of migrant organisations in Berlin's integration policy is the State Advisory Board on Migration and Integration (*Landesbeirat für Integrations- und Migrationsfragen*). Since 2010, the Board has a legal standing in Berlin's Integration and Participation law. The Board is composed of seven representatives from migrant associations as well as several city and district officials. The representatives from migrant associations are elected in a public meeting by registered migrant organisations. The Advisory Board has agenda-setting powers and is tasked with developing recommendations, which are later directed to the Senate and stakeholder-associations, but it has no direct policy formulation powers. The Board also has to approve the appointment of Berlin commissioners for migration and integration. It meets four times per year under the leadership of the senator for Integration, Labour, and Social Affairs.

Experience sharing with other subnational governments and peer-learning

The city of Berlin engages in many peer-learning activities. As a member of the German Day of Cities (*Deutscher Staedtetag*), it exchanges with other German cities on a regular basis about measures regarding immigration, integration and refugees. Additionally Berlin is a member of the "Communal Circle on quality in Integration Policy" (*Kommunaler Qualitaetszirkel zur Inetgrationspolitik*) that facilitates exchange of good practices on integration among local commissioners for integration as well as research institutions, foundations and the Ministry of Interior (BMI). On integration matters, the city also exchanges at international level through the Cities Twinning programme of which it has been member since 1990. Additional cooperation exists in related policy fields, for instance through European associations of subnational governments such as Eurocities.

Communicating on integration with the public opinion

Berlin perceives itself as a city of diversity that has challenges but also benefits. This is clearly stated in communications with its citizens. The municipality implemented an advertising campaign to encourage the foreign-born to undertake the necessary steps towards naturalisation. In addition, it supported a campaign targeting employers encouraging them to hire refugees, publishing billboards with the slogan "Refugee is not a job". In the information material produced for refugees and asylum seekers since 2015, the Mayor welcomes them in the name of the city of Berlin, wishing they can find their place there.

Key data on migrant presence and integration in Berlin

Figure 1. Berlin localisation in Germany according to OCED regional classification

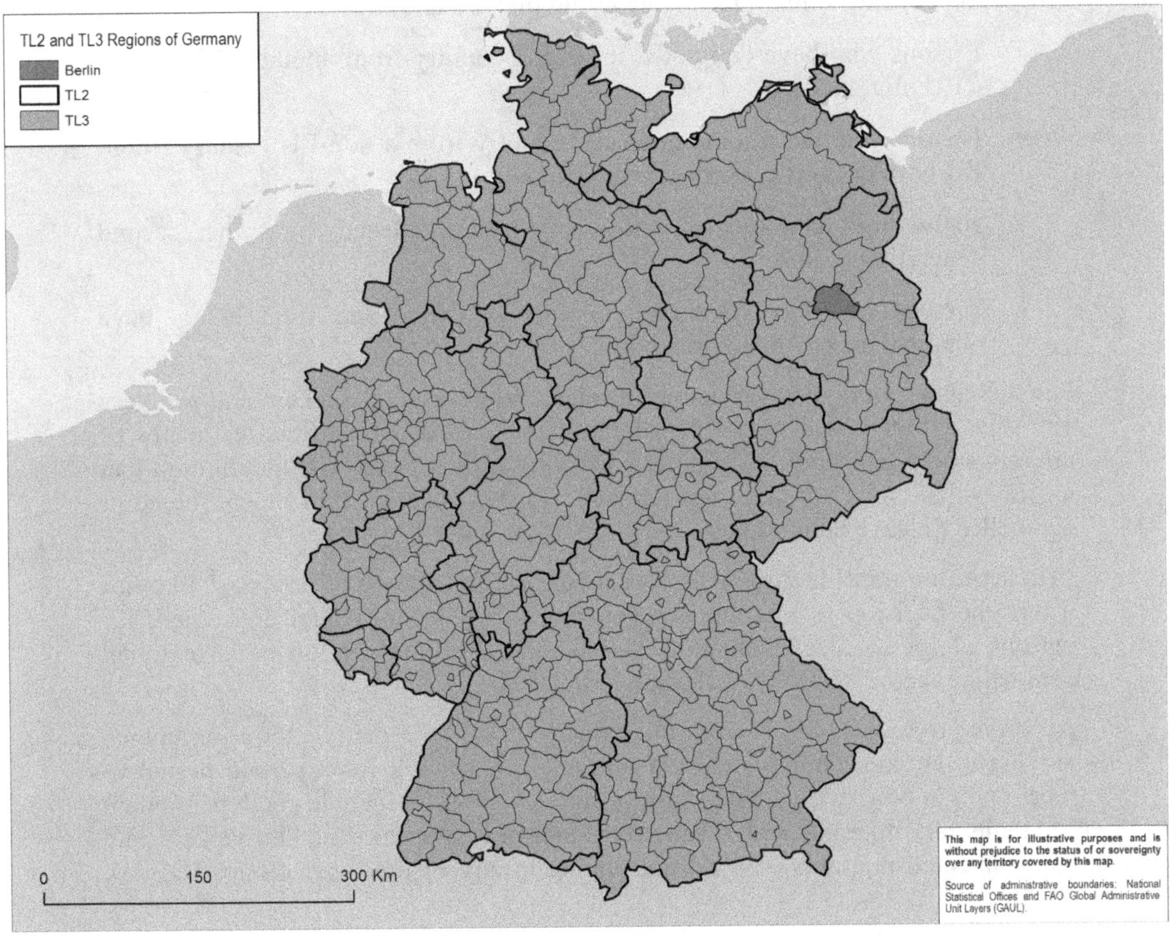

Note: TL2 (Territorial Level 2) consists of the OECD classification of regions within each member country. There are 335 regions classified at this level across 35 member countries. In Germany the TL2 Level corresponds to the Lander governance level. There are 16 Lander at TL2 Level in Germany. TL3 (Territorial Level 3) consists of the lower level of classification and is composed of 1 681 small regions. In most cases, they correspond to administrative regions. There are 96 Spatial Planning Regions at TL2 level in Germany.
Source: OECD (2018), OECD Regional Statistics (database), http://dx.doi.org/10.1787/region-data-en.

Box 1. Definition of migrant

The term "migrant" generally functions as an umbrella term used to describe people that move to another country with the intention of staying for a significant period of time. According to the United Nations (UN), a long-term migrant is "a person who moves to a country other than that of his or her usual residence for a period of at least a year (12 months)" (UNSD, 2017). Yet, not all migrants move for the same reasons, have the same needs or are subject to the same laws.

This report considers migrants a large group that includes:

- Persons who have emigrated to an EU country from another EU country ('EU migrants'),

- Persons who have come to an EU country from a non-EU country ('non-EU born or third-country national'),

- Native-born children of immigrants (often referred to as the 'second generation'), and

- Persons who have fled their country of origin and are seeking/ have obtained international protection.

For the latter, some distinctions are needed. While asylum seekers and refugees are often counted as a subset of migrants and included in official estimates of migrant stocks and flows, this is not correct according to the UN's definition that indicates that "migrant" does not refer to refugees, displaced, or others forced or compelled to leave their homes:

"The term 'migrant' in Article 1.1 (a) should be understood as covering all cases where the decision to migrate is taken freely by the individual concerned, for reasons of 'personal convenience' and without the intervention of an external compelling factor" (IOM Constitution Article 1.1 (a)).

According to recent OECD work the term "migrant" is a generic term for anyone moving to another country with the intention of staying for a certain period of time – not, in other words, tourists or business visitors. It includes both permanent and temporary migrants with a valid residence permit or visa, asylum seekers, and undocumented migrants who do not belong to any of the three groups (OECD, 2016b).

Thus, in this report the following terms are used:

- "Status holder" or "refugee" who have successfully applied for asylum and have been granted some sort of protection in their host country, including those who are recognised on the basis of the 1951 Geneva Convention Relating to the Status of Refugees, but also those benefiting from national asylum laws or EU legislation (Directive 2011/95/EU), such as the subsidiary protection status. This corresponds to the category 'humanitarian migrants' meaning recipients of protection – be it refugee status, subsidiarity or temporary protection – as used in recent OECD work (OECD, 2016b).

- 'Asylum seeker' for those individuals who have submitted a claim for international protection but are awaiting the final decision.

- 'Rejected asylum seeker' for those individuals who have been denied protection status.

- 'Undocumented or irregular migrants' for those who do not have a legal permission to stay.

This report systematically distinguishes which group is targeted by policies and services put in place by the city. Where statistics provided by the cities included refugees in the migrant stocks and flows, it will be indicated accordingly.

In the case of Berlin, the term migrant includes all those who were not born with German nationality and those individuals who have at least one migrant parent born without German nationality. This is generally specified as 'having a migration background'. Further, Berlin's statistics do not differentiate between asylum seekers and refugees.

Key Statistics[1]

- City composition - # of districts: 12

- Growth of GDP 2016: 2.7%, Germany: 1.9%

- Total city population: 3 485 900[2]

- % of the population with a migration background: 27.7%, (federal average: 21%)

- The most important countries of origin of residents with foreign passport: Turkey (174 505), Poland (106 889) Russian Federation (49 912), Italy (32 887), Serbia (27,885)[3]

- Number of registered Asylum seekers[4]: 2013 – 6 100 , 2015 – 33 300, 2016 – 27 247

Employment and Labour

Main industrial sectors where people with a migration background work:[5]

- 32.6% Wholesale and retail trade; repair of motor vehicles and motorcycles, Transportation and storage, Accommodation and food service activities

- 23.1% Information and communication, Financial and insurance activities, Real estate activities, Professional, scientific and technical activities, Administrative and support service activities

Full time employment:

Berlin: Migration Background	Berlin: No-migration background	Federal Average Migration Background	Federal Average No migration background
54.6%	74.4%	64.6%	76.3%

Unemployed:

Berlin: Migration Background	Berlin: No-migration background	Federal Average Migration Background	Federal Average No migration background
17.1%	7.2%	7.8%	4%

Apprenticeships in Berlin (18-21 year olds):

Migration background female	No migration background female	Migration background male	No migration background male
4%	16.8%	4.8%	21.3%

Self-employed:

Berlin Migration Background	Berlin No-migration background	Federal Average Migration Background	Federal Average No migration background
20.5%	15.0%	10.0 %	10.3%

Population at risk of poverty in Berlin (share of people to general population, whose income is below the threshold for risk of poverty):

- People with a migration background: 28.1%, people without a migration background 10.6%

Education

Educational Attainment in Berlin (primary, secondary, tertiary)

Migrant Population				Non-migrant population			
Primary	Secondary	Tertiary	University degree after enrolment	Primary	Secondary	Tertiary	University degree after enrolment
15.9%	41.1%	20.2 %	62.3%	2.6%	58.4%	29.5%	81.8%

Source: Statistical Office of Berlin-Brandenberg (2017).

Housing

Personal living space (in m²) / Families (with children under 18) per Person:

Berlin: Migration Background	Berlin: No-migration background	Federal Average Migration Background	Federal Average No migration background
21.8m²	29.5m²	25.9m²	34.1m²

Political Participation

Right to vote: EU and federal constitutional law provide EU citizens the right to vote in district elections. The basis for that is the EU citizenship. All other migrants do not have the right to vote.

Notes

[1] * Numbers and percentages are provided by the Integrationsmonitoring of the Länder (2016). Data covers the period of 2013-2015, unless stated otherwise. The source includes people in the group "people with a migration background" who either 1. are foreigners, 2. are born abroad and moved to Germany after 31.12.1955, 3. have at least one parent who was born abroad and moved to Germany after 31.12.1995 (For the whole definition please refer to References "Integrationsmonitoring der Länder 2016").

[2] Berlin Municipality (2017).

[3] Ibid.

[4] Ibid.

[5] Ibid.

Introduction

The objective of this case study is to analyse refugee and migrant integration policy in Berlin. The study highlights the design and implementation of integration actions within the German multi-level governance framework for integration, as well as interactions between the municipality and other public and non-state stakeholders. The study is based on different sources of information: a questionnaire filled out by the municipality of Berlin and its partners, interviews conducted during the OECD mission (8-9 March 2017) and complementary responses, and existing data and literature.

This report takes as a starting point a multi-dimensional definition of integration:

> *The effective integration of migrants is not an economic and labour-market process alone. It also has social, educational – even spatial – facets. None, though, are mutually exclusive: disadvantage and the failure to integrate in one dimension are likely to have multiple repercussions. Concentrations of migrants in geographically disadvantaged areas, for example, may affect effective integration in the education system and, later, the labour market (OECD/EU, 2015).*

Berlin is both, one of the federal states (Länder) and a municipality, providing it with state rights and competencies when dealing with migration. Thus the scope of analysis of this case study includes state policies as well as city policies as they are valid for an identical geographical territory.

Berlin is a city that has been attracting people from all over the world for decades. Many of the workers recruited from abroad during the economic boom in the 1950s, 60s and 70s were commonly called 'guest workers', indicating the expectation that they would return to their home countries after work contracts expired. During that time, municipalities, cities and third sector entities engaged as key actors in diverging paths towards access to labour, education, participation and intercultural opening in Germany (Gesemann, 2001). In 1970 West Berlin installed the first "Committee to Coordinate Assistance to Foreign Workers" and two years later the Senate commissioned an interdepartmental working party within the city government to look into the "integration of foreign workers and their families" (Mahnig, 2004). A little later it institutionalised migration and integration questions through the role of the Commissioner for integration and migration, in 1980. This was just shortly after the first federal institution, the administrative office of a Commissioner for the Affairs of the Foreign Population (Auslaenderbeauftragter), was created in 1978 (OECD, 2007). Overall, Berlin's polices preceded the federal level in the creation of a comprehensive integration policy roughly twenty five years, as the federal government advanced on this only in the beginning of the 2000s (Hübschmann, 2015; Bendel, 2014; OECD, 2007). It emerged from OECD interviews with city officers that Berlin's first integration concepts even served as a role model in the development of the first federal National Integration Plan in mid-2000. Today, the city tries to establish itself as a city where diversity, not only with regard to nationality, is perceived as an asset and widely accepted in society. This study focuses on the engagement in Integration policy making in Berlin – for an analysis of integration concepts in Germany and Berlin please see 2.4.4.Annex B of this study.

The study is structured as follows. First, migration and refugee inflows to Germany and the city of Berlin are sketched and key laws concerning immigration and access to services for migrant groups are outlined. In the subsequent section well-being and the others indicators regarding integration of migrants in Berlin are described. The second part of the study analyses responses to these issues according to the objectives identified in the OECD *Checklist for public action to migrant integration at the local level*. The first block presents responses in the allocation of competencies across the multi-level governance framework of the Federal Republic. In the following chapter city responses are presented in their efforts to create proximity and continuity over time. The third block depicts monitoring and operational tools for migrant integration and the following block presents solutions in the sectors of labour market, education, housing and social service. Finally, the concluding chapter will reflect on the findings and identify best practices to be replicated elsewhere.

1. Migration snapshot of the city of Berlin

1.1. Migration insights: flows, stock and nationalities

Berlin is a growing city; each year, its population increases by around 48 000 people. At the time of writing, Berlin holds over 180 nationalities and nearly one-third (27.7%) of the population has a migration background[1] (federal average: 21%)[2].

The history of Berlin has been connected to migration for several centuries. In the 17th and 18th century the city offered refugee to French Huguenots (Protestants who were persecuted in mostly catholic France) and later was characterised by immigration from more eastern regions of Prussia. After the Second World War and the division of Berlin in four occupation zones, policies regarding immigration were shaped by the two opposed ideologies (Gesemann, 2006: 197). Migration to eastern Berlin was largely controlled and regulated. Starting in the 1950s, Germany and western Berlin reacted to the declining population with ample measures and programmes to expand the industrial private sector by recruiting low-skilled and cheap labour - the "Guest workers" (OECD, 2007; Gesemann, 2006: 198). People who came to Berlin through this recruitment process, mainly originated from Turkey and Yugoslavia (Gesemann, 2006: 198)[3].

After the oil crisis in 1973 the western federal government imposed a ban on recruitment. As a consequence around 11 million of the 14 million who arrived during the period left the country. The immigration pattern to Germany and western Berlin thereby shifted from labour-orientation to family reunification (Federal Commisioner for Migration, Refugees and Integration, 2016: 24). Another group that has shaped the immigration discourse in Germany and Berlin since the early 1950s are ethnic Germans (*Aussiedler and Spätaussiedler[4]*), coming from previously German territories (OECD, 2007). The influx of repatriates reached a peak with the fall of the Berlin Wall and the disintegration of the Soviet Union. The group consists mainly of nationals from the former Soviet Union, Poland and Romania.

In the late 1980s, due to political tension and violent conflicts in Eastern Europe, Germany as well as Berlin experienced a large inflow of people seeking asylum especially from the former Soviet Union, Poland and Yugoslavia, as well as Kurdish refugees from Iraq and Turkey (OECD, 2007).

By 1989 around 4.9 million people with a foreign background lived in Germany (Federal Office for Migration and Refugees, 2015: 13). In 2015, approximately 11.5 million foreign-born and 9.1 million foreigners were living in Germany (OECD, 2017d).

**Figure 1.1. Most important countries of origin of people
with migration background in Berlin, 2015**

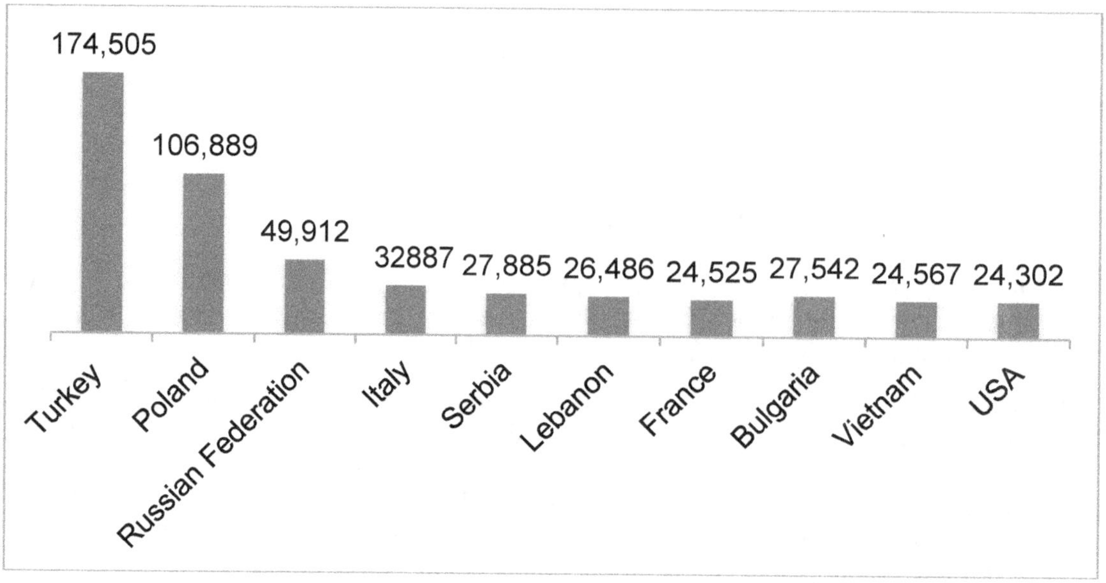

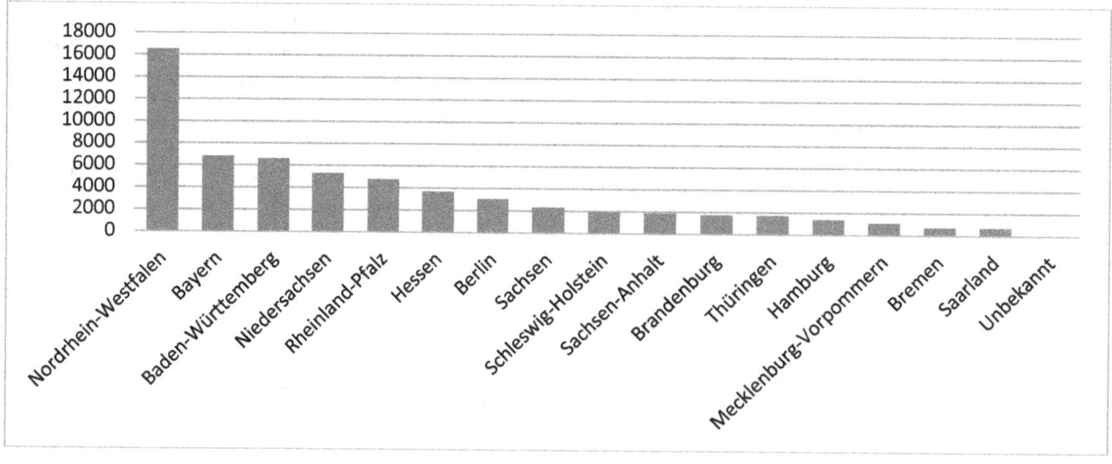

Source: Author's elaboration based on Statistical Office of Berlin-Brandenberg (2015), A I 5 hj 2 / 15, S. 18-25 (database).

Berlin received around 5% of all refugees coming to Germany: in 2015 well over 50 000 asylum seekers were registered in the city. This number sharply decreased to 16 889 asylum seekers in 2016 and 6 770 asylum seekers in 2017 and 720 in January 2018 (Landesamt für Flüchtlingsangelegenheiten, 2017). Berlin does not receive the highest number of asylum seekers in Germany or the highest number of asylum applications (see Figure 1.2 below for distribution across Länder in Germany).

Figure 1.2. Asylum Applications per Land in Germany, 2017

Source: Federal Office for Migration and Refugees (Bundesamt für Migration und Flüchtlinge, BAMF).

Against this background, Berlin's migration pattern is now mostly framed by intra-European migration: out of the 33 587 people who move to the city in 2015, 15 543 of immigrants came from European countries and 11 206 originated from an EU member state (Statistical Office of Berlin-Brandenberg).

The gender distribution of Berlin's migrant population is quite equal between men (50.5%) and women (49.4%). Berlin is both a city of transit and (mainly) a city of destination for migrants: 43.2% of its current migrant population have been residing in the city for longer than 10 years and 33.2% were born in Germany but have at least one parent who was born abroad, while 15.7% of the group stayed less than 5 years in Berlin. Berlin's migrant population is quite young: more than half (54.7%) are less than 35 years old, from which 26.7% are under 18 years old. Only 7% are retirees (over 65).

1.2. City well-being and inclusion

According to an ad hoc analysis of the OECD dataset, overall well-being in Berlin (Lander) is quite different from the German average. Berlin is underperforming in seven of the eleven dimensions: education, jobs, income, safety, environment, housing and life satisfaction. On the contrary, Berlin is outperforming in health, civic engagement, accessibility to services and sense of community.

Figure 1.3. Well-being dataset of Berlin

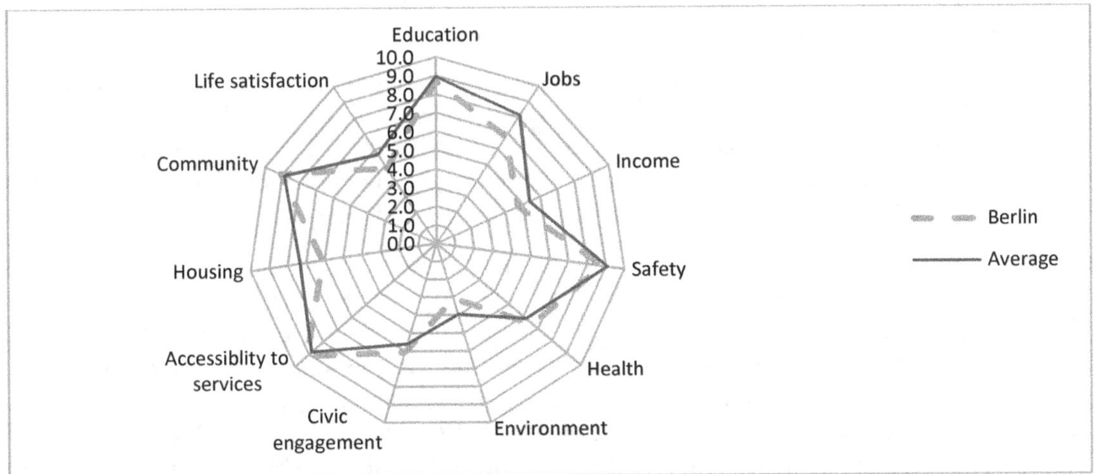

Source: Ad hoc elaboration based on OECD regional well-being dataset.

Since the reunification of Germany, Berlin's labour market has been generally characterised by high unemployment in comparison to the federal average (Gesemann, 2006: 202; IHK Berlin, 2012: 5). As a reaction to the economic structural changes, Berlin's population declined and was shaped by an emigration pattern to its surrounding regions (Parliament Berlin, 2014: 3). After the unemployment rate reached a peak of 19% in 2005, it began to decline and the population began to expand steadily again (IHK Berlin, 2016a: 10). Since then, Berlin has started to establish itself as a metropolis of science, innovation and technology. The prestigious research and science institutions located in the city, such as well-known universities or the establishment of the biggest Science and Technology Park in Germany in Berlin (Adlershof), has contributed to the change (IHK, 2012:5). Over 250 000 new jobs were created, mainly in science, technology, creative industry and knowledge-based services (Berlin Municipality, 2014). Additionally Berlin is a growing centre for the start-up scene in Europe. The number of enterprises created in the city exceeds the number of shuttered ones by far (IHK Berlin,

2016a: 6). In 2015 about 62% of the employees worked in the SME sector. Since 2005 Berlin's economic growth rate has exceeded the overall national growth (2016: B 2.7%, G 1.9%) according to Statistische Ämter des Bundes und der Länder.

Berlin's economic recovery, affordable rents and available space as well as its reputation as a creative and entrepreneurial hub during the last decade, has attracted many (young and also high-skilled) people from all over the world whether it is for work or to study (Malorny, Raderschall and Werner, 2016; IHK Berlin, 2012: 5). The number of people with a migration background has likewise increased. In the past 5 years Berlin grew from 3 517 424 inhabitants to the currently around 3 710 000. The net-migration balance, including foreign-born and native people, has shown a steady inflow since 2007. While in 2011, +24 000 (2011) came to live in Berlin it was already +43 000 in 2015 (The Berlin Commissioner for Migration and Integration; Amt für Statitstik Berlin Brandenburg). In this regard, Berlin presents a special case compared to other areas and cities in the country and draws its attractiveness mainly from its international image as a lively, innovative, creative and multicultural city, with a reasonably low cost of living. Furthermore, the city became an attractive destination, especially in the years after the fall of the Berlin wall, for tourism, which is an industry that has been growing markedly in recent decades (Pfeffer-Hoffmann, 2016: 9). In this regard, the city's commissioner for migration and integration perceives diversity as generally accepted in Berlin's society [5]. Yet, in 2016 local elections the party that criticizes immigration[6] entered the Berlin Parliament for the first time.

The sharp population growth however, also presents challenges, in particular regarding its infrastructure and capacities of administration, schools, childcare facilities or access to (social) housing. Even though many efforts are made, the building of infrastructure, especially to meet housing needs, but also school and childcare facilities, in Berlin has been generally lagging behind extensive growth rates (Sueddeutsche.de, 2016).

People with a migration background in particular have been and are continuously impacted by economic structural changes. In Berlin, the share of people in the age group 18-21 years with a migration background who participated in a dual apprenticeship[7] is only one fourth (female: 5.4%, male: 4.8%) as high as the share of people without a migration background within the same age group (female: 16.8%, male: 21.3%) according to Integrationsmonitoring der Länder (2017). The majority of Berlin's migrant population is registered as students (26.2%), followed by full-time employed (25.2%) and part-time employed (13.7%) according to Berlin Municipality (2017).

Some areas of Berlin are socio-economically weaker, which is reflected in higher (long-term) unemployment and child poverty rates (Berlin Senate, 2015: 11). There are also strong concentrations of migrations in certain areas of Berlin. Owing to its historical legacy as a divided city after WWII until the disintegration of the Soviet Union, Berlin is different from other parts of Germany and other metropolises. With the expansion of the city after the fall of the Berlin Wall, the former suburbs became the new centre. While in some cities migrant populations are largely situated on the outskirts of the city, the share of people with a migration background is higher in some areas of the centre of the city than in its suburbs. There is a strong correspondence between deprived areas in the centre of the city and the percentage of foreign born/native population, in particular in Wedding (part of district Mitte), North-east district Kreuzberg and in the North of Neukölln. Native-born people of migrant parents are underrepresented in socio-economically strong areas on the city's outskirts and averagely represented in deprived outskirt areas (Berlin Senate, 2015).

Settlements of migrant groups as well as native-born people of migrant parents in distinct neighbourhoods are in general motivated by cheaper housing prices and availability of social housing as well as the presence of relatives and incumbent community presence. For the allocation of people with a migration background in the city see Figure 1.4.

**Figure 1.4. Percentage of population with migration background
above the age of 18 per district, Berlin, 2017**

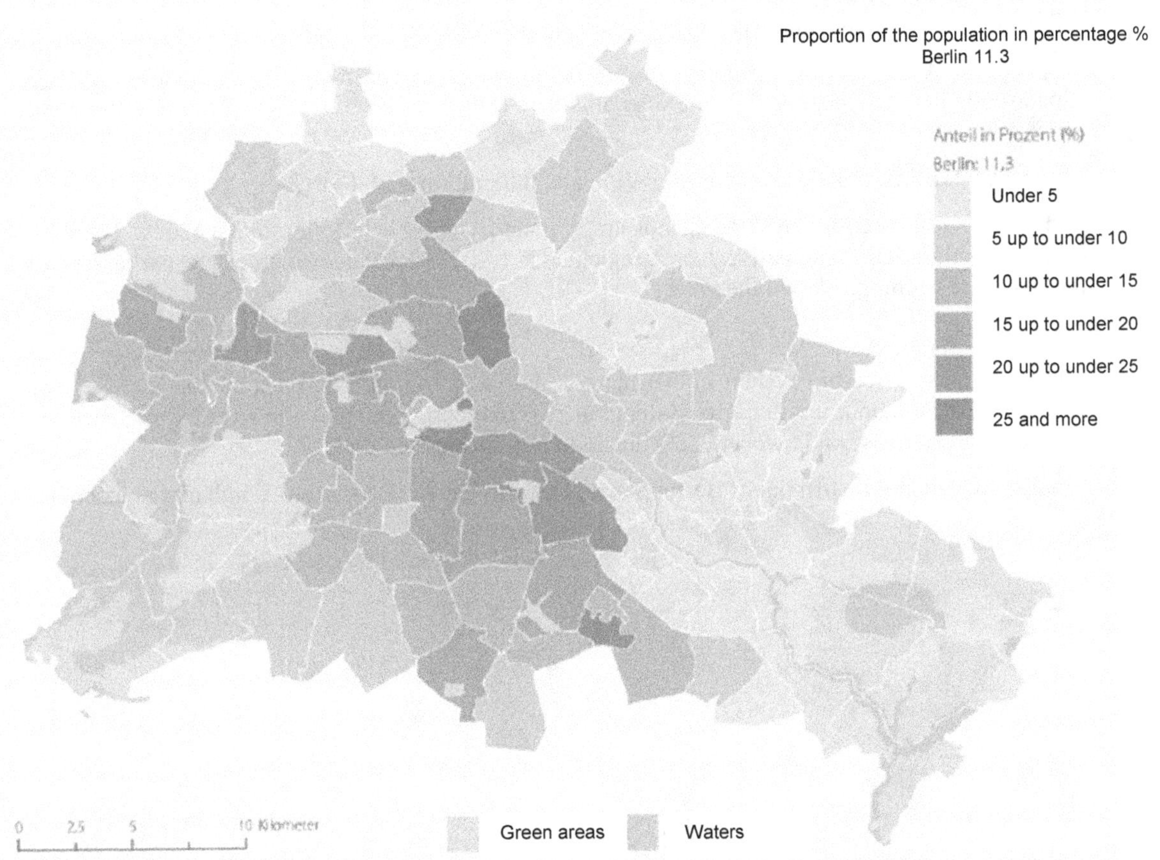

Note: Population with migration background: Share of the population who were born abroad/foreign nationals or at least one of their parents was born abroad or has foreign nationalities.
Source: Statistical Office of Berlin-Brandenburg (2017).

In terms of educational segregation, Berlin's school system foresees that children attend school close to the place of residence. Allocation of newly arrived students is subject to availability. As a result of spatial concentration of migrant groups in some areas of the city, as mentioned above, some schools experience particularly high percentages of migrant children[8]. Migrant children in Berlin in general achieve weaker educational results than their native peers (see Key indicators above). Previous OECD research pointed to a linkage of educational attainment of children, with their socio-economic background (OECD, 2010). The poverty risk in Berlin for people with a migration background, at 28.1%, is nearly three times higher than for people without (10.6%) according to Integrationsmonitoring der Länder (2017).

Notes

[1] The concept of having a migration background was introduced in Germany in 2002. It includes people who have at least one parent with a non-German foreign background in the last two generations (Hübschmann, 2015: 14)

[2] Data based on Berlin Municipality (2017).

[3] On average in Germany most migrants coming to the country at the time originated from Italy, followed by Turkey and Yugoslavia (for details see Höhne et al., 2014: 5).

[4] The term 'Aussiedler' is used for those who migrated to Germany before January 1, 1993; 'Spätasussiedler' for those who came after this date (Federal Office for Migration and Refugees, 2015: 13).

[5] Interview Berlin commissioner for migration and integration on 8 March 2017.

[6] The past local elections in 2016 demonstrate a sharp increase in migration sceptics. The party critical of migration "Alternative fuer Deutschland" (AfD) succeeded to enter the parliament for the first time winning, 14% of the votes.

https://www.wahlen-berlin.de/wahlen/BU2017/AllgemInfo.asp?sel1=2156&sel2=1000.

[7] The dual apprenticeship system in Germany is the most common entry point for young people into the German labour market. The system has two main components: a practical experience in a company or enterprise and a vocational education in a specialised college.

[8] Interview with public official of Berlin Senate Department for Education, Youth and Science.

2. The Checklist for public action on migrant integration at the local level applied to the city of Berlin

This section is structured following the Checklist for public action to migrant integration at the local level, as included in the Synthesis Report (OECD, 2018) which comprises a list of 12 evidence-based objectives that can be used by policy makers and practitioners in the development and implementation of migrant integration programmes, at local, regional, national and international levels. This Checklist highlights for the first time common messages and cross-cutting lessons learnt around policy frameworks, institutions, and mechanisms that feature in policies for migrant and refugee integration.

This innovative tool has been elaborated by the OECD as part of the larger study on "Working Together for Local Integration of Migrants and Refugees" supported by the European Commission, Directorate General for regional and urban policies. The Checklist is articulated according to four blocks and 12 objectives. This part describes the actions implemented in Berlin following this framework.

Checklist for Public Action to Migrant Integration at the Local Level

Block 1. Multi-level governance: Institutional and financial settings

Objective 1. Enhance the effectiveness of migrant integration policy through improved vertical co-ordination and implementation at the relevant scale.

Objective 2. Seek policy coherence in addressing the multi-dimensional needs of, and opportunities for, migrants at the local level.

Objective 3. Ensure access to, and effective use of, financial resources that are adapted to local responsibilities for migrant integration.

Block 2. Time and space: Keys for migrants and host communities to live together

Objective 4. Design integration policies that take time into account throughout migrants' lifetimes and evolution of residency status.

Objective 5. Create spaces where the interaction brings migrant and native-born communities closer.

Block 3. Local capacity for policy formulation and implementation

Objective 6. Build capacity and diversity in civil service, with a view to ensuring access to mainstream services for migrants and newcomers.

Objective 7. Strengthen co-operation with non-state stakeholders, including through transparent and effective contracts.

Objective 8. Intensify the assessment of integration results for migrants and host communities and their use for evidence-based policies.

Block 4. Sectoral policies related to integration

Objective 9. Match migrant skills with economic and job opportunities.

Objective 10. Secure access to adequate housing.

Objective 11. Provide social welfare measures that are aligned with migrant inclusion.

Objective 12. Establish education responses to address segregation and provide equitable paths to professional growth.

2.1. Block 1 Multi-level governance: Institutional and financial settings

2.1.1. *Objective 1. Enhance effectiveness of migrant integration policy through improved vertical co-ordination and implementation at the relevant scale.*

Division of competences across levels of government

Berlin is one of three city-states in Germany. Its governmental structure fulfils functions of a Land and a city as the same time, increasing its leverage in designing and implementing policies compared to other German cities. While the federal government is largely responsible for setting the legal framework for integration and migration, e.g. regulating residency permits, nationality and free movement as well as access to labour market and access to language courses (Bendel 2014: 5, Leptien, 2014; OECD, 2017b), the Länder enjoy specific legislative competences in the areas of education policy, culture and the relational economy. Together with municipalities, the Länder are in charge of implementing federal laws, which provides them with considerable leeway in implementing policy. Overall, three modes of jurisdictional schemes exist: Areas under strictly federal authority, shared right to legislate, and areas were only *Länder* have the right to pass legislation. Shared legislation is of relevance for *Länder* in all areas where the federal level does not make use of its right to draft legislation. This is the case for all policies like youth, welfare and labour affairs. In practice however most areas under shared legislation already contain federal regulations. For a distribution of competencies at the federal, Länder and district level, please refer to the table in Annex C.

Allocation of competences for specific migration-related matters

Figure 2.1. Multilevel Institutional Mapping for migrant integration

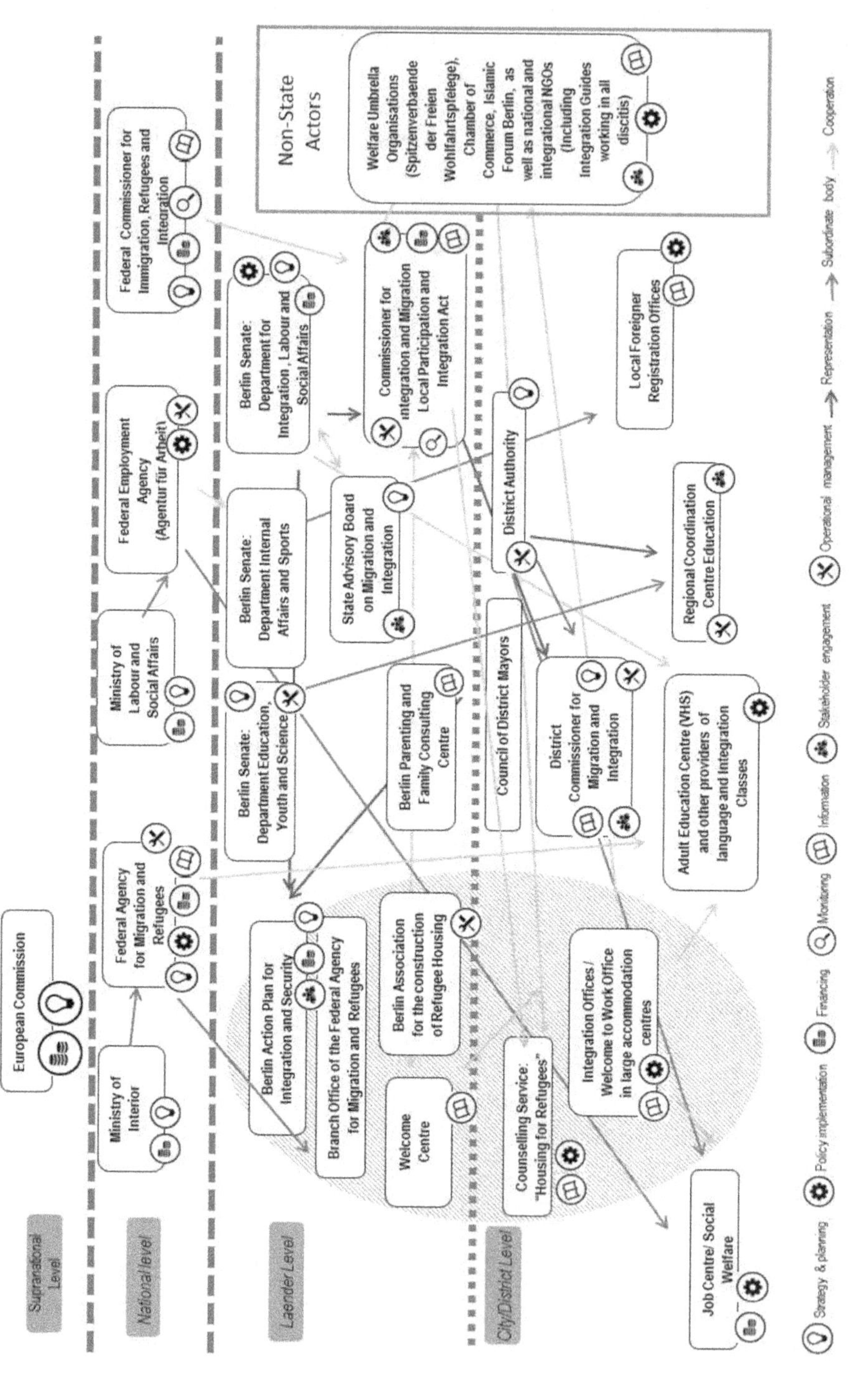

Source: Author's elaboration.

On the federal level several bodies hold responsibilities in the field of migrant integration: The Ministry of the Interior, Building and Community (BMI) and its executive Federal Office for Migration and Refugees (Bundesamt für Migration und Flüchtlinge, BAMF). In the field of labour integration the Federal Ministry for Labour and Social Affairs (BMAS) which supervises the Federal Employment Agency. The Federal Commissioner for Migration, Refugees, and Integration situated within the Chancellery. Besides, further Ministries conduct programs or are in charge of integration-related legislation as a cross-sectional task, such as the Federal Ministry of Education and Research, the Federal Ministry of Family Affairs, Senior Citizens, Women and Youth. Through their subsidiary bodies the formerly named BMI and BMAS are engaged in policy implementation at the regional and local level.

The BMI has central powers in the policy area of integration, it has jurisdiction in drafting legislation regarding immigration, refugee protection and citizenship and grants funding to integration projects in the Länder, and at the local level. The subordinate BAMF centralises two important implementation tasks related to migration and integration, assessing asylum applications and supporting the integration of migrants through the design and implementation of federation-wide integration courses at the local level (OECD, 2017b). Therefore, one common agency was put in charge of implementing federal law in their scope of responsibility nation-wide, with several sub-offices across *Länder* and municipalities that exchange locally with non-state organisations operating in integration activities.

The Integration Courses' main goal is to teach basic language skills, but also orientation and guidance in administrative procedures as well as German culture, history and the country's legal system. To carry out the courses, local private and public entities, like adult education centres are contracted (Bendel, 2014: 7; Federal Office for Migration and Refugees, 2016: 16). In Berlin, 123 contracted educational entities implement these courses, listed in the so-called Kursnet – a platform of the Federal Employment Agency (see below).

The Federal Ministry of Labour and Social Affairs (BMAS) is in charge of measures for the integration of migrants in the labour market. The BMAS supervises the subordinated Federal Employment Agency (*Bundesagentur für Arbeit)*, which is mainly responsible for implementing regional labour market policies such as the (re-) integration of people into the labour market. The Agency administers the unemployment insurance and respective financial welfare mechanisms. The Federal Employment Agency has 10 regional offices (*Regionaldirektion*) and 156 Employment agencies at the local level. The employment agency is responsible for the integration of asylum seekers, while refugees are supported by the Jobcenters. Locally, Jobcenters are either run by municipalities themselves or in cooperation with the Employment Agency. They are responsible for allocating social welfare contributions and implementing measures regarding labour force activation.

The Minister of State in the Federal Chancellery and Federal Government Commissioner for Migration, Refugees and Integration are heavily involved in the design, co-ordination and evaluation of the federal integration strategy, the National Action Plan for Integration (2012). The plan is the result of steady changes made to the first National Integration Plan introduced in 2007. It includes a comprehensive framework in the areas of education, labour market, sports, arts, media, as well as regional integration (for more information see 2.4.4.Annex B). The plan demonstrates just how important integration is at the national level. It is largely inspired by other levels of government and non-state actors operating at local level. Since 2005, the Commissioner for Migration, Refugees and

Integration has been affiliated in the federal Chancellery with a subordinated portfolio and its own budget. The budget of the commissioner in 2015 was EUR 5 million. In 2016 and 2017 an additional EUR 20 million was added to it. The commissioner directly funds projects that relate to specific topics such as education and labour, society and participation, asylum and refugees, as well as research. Further the office publishes a bi-yearly report on Migration, Integration and Refugees and the progress made based on integration indicators.

At the subnational level, under Länder jurisdiction, (in Berlin affiliated with the Senate Department of Interior and Sports) are 570 Foreigners Registration Offices where rights of residence and visa credentials are issued, deciding whether people are entitled to work permits or not. Further, the Foreigners Registration Offices cooperates with private actors, such as the chamber of commerce and private companies in facilitating the recruitment of workforce. In Berlin, the Foreigners Registration Office has a central office in Berlin – Mitte working directly under the Berlin Senate Department for Internal Affairs and Sports.

Integration-related national-local co-ordination mechanisms

The development of the National Integration Plan (2005), and the National Action Plan for Integration in 2012, represented an important step in the co-ordination of integration policymaking. *Länder,* as well as cities and towns, contributed to its development, comprising more than 400 measures and commitments providing local and state officials with objectives for migrant integration. *Länder* and cities contributed to the plan with their own chapters (Bendel, 2014). Further, they committed themselves to adhering to common guidelines and coordinated procedures introduced by national frameworks, mainly in the areas of language learning and education (Bundesregierung, 2007). Overall, the plan aims to promote closer co-ordination and networking across levels and recognizes integration as a cross-cutting policy task also involving non-state stakeholders. Progress on measures and commitments on all levels of government is verified through annual reports published by the federal government.

Co-ordination among Lander and the Federal Government

As a *Land*, Berlin takes part in all the co-ordination and representation that takes place amongst *Länder* and between the *Länder* and the federal government. The two conferences (mentioned below) between *Länder* and federal level are examples that complement the regular cooperation of *Länder* in the lower chamber, the Bundesrat, on legislative and administrative matters. The Bundesrat also holds a committee on Work, Integration and Social Policy.

The creation of the National Integration Plan also resulted from the institutionalised dialogue conference of ministers for integration of the *Länder* (*Integrationsministerministerkonferenz,* IntMK) which was established in 2006 to coordinate regions' actions on a voluntary basis. Once a year, the 16 ministers responsible for integration affairs come together to discuss recent challenges in the field of integration and migration. The conference is also an interface with the federal level, since the lander ministers often present their needs to the federal level. Usually the Land holding the chair decides on a guiding topic and sets the agenda. Participating Länder also constitute work groups and prepare reports on those topics. One example is the working group on integration monitoring (länderoffene Arbeitsgruppe Integrationsmonitoring). In addition to the conference, the IntMK publishes a state integration monitoring report

(*Integrationsmonitioring der Länder*) on a biannual basis, which is an important set of indicators measuring various dimensions of social integration compared across *Länder*. Indicators are based on data from the micro census (a yearly survey of roughly 380 000 households covering 820 000 persons in Germany). Integration is measured in important areas such as education, employment, health or housing. Each *Land* contributes and delivers data to the working group of *Länder* experts, Ministers and Senators.

Depending on the Land, the roles of Integration Minister and the Commissioner for Integration and Foreigners can be held by the same person. This is not the case in Berlin, where 'Senator for Integration, Labour and Social Policy' and the 'Commissioner of the Senate for Migration and Integration' are two different positions working in the same ministry.

A second conference aiming to better coordinate Lander policy is the Permanent Conference of Ministers and Senators for the Interior of the federal Lander (Innenministerkonferenz, IMK). It takes place twice a year and is an important venue for coordinating policy making between *Länder* and the federal level. Exchange here is mostly concerned with aspects pertaining to residence and asylum rights, which is again implemented by the Foreign Registration Offices of the *Länder*. The Minister of Interior participates in an advisory role. Whilst these measures of exchange and alignment seem to be important to increase co-ordination and communication between *Länder* and the federal level there is a consensus in the literature that across *Länder* integration policy differs considerably (Gesemann/Roth, 2015: 22; Bendel, 2014). This largely stems from the fact that 1) Lander hold competences on integration matters that they implement differently and 2) federal laws give leeway in interpretation of national law.

Co-ordination involving the local level

In its capacity as a city, Berlin is a member of the German Day of Cities (Deutscher Städtetag) an organisation created to represent the interest of cities and towns at *Länder*, Federal and EU level. It also aims to facilitate information exchange. It is one of three head organisations that represent the interest of the local level, the other two are the German Day of Counties (Deutscher Landkreistag) and the German Association of Towns and Municipalities (Deutscher Städte- und Gemeindebund). The importance of national associations of local and regional governments in co-ordination of multi-level governance for migrant integration is not only relevant for Berlin but was further underlined by many large and small German cities like Düsseldorf, Freising, Karlsruhe, Schwarbach that were consulted for the OECD report "A Territorial Approach to Migrant Integration".

Membership in the German Day of Cities is voluntary, but most municipalities participate. The umbrella organisation is funded by the contributions of its members, hence is independent and not entitled to its own assigned budget by the federal or *Länder* level. It does not enjoy a right to appeal *Länder* and federal decisions, but largely communicates and coordinates activities vertically between the federal (i.e. *Länder*) and municipal level.

In addition, there are other venues that are important in the context of integration, which take place on a smaller scale. For instance, public officials representing immigration authorities in areas with high population density, meet twice each year for experience exchange (Federal Office for Migration and Refugees, 2016: 14).

Border Co-ordination Mechanisms that span across all levels of government are rather scarce. One of them is the yearly integration summit (Integrationsgipfel), convened by the Chancellery, which brings together a broad variety of stakeholders, including different government levels and non-state actors. Yet, representation from local level has been rather limited in recent years. Overall, Berlin (thanks to its dual status as a city and a Land) seems to be well integrated into a variety of co-ordination mechanisms that allow for exchange with the federal government – mostly due to its roles as a Land – but also with other Länder as well as other municipalities. Nevertheless the impact of these exchanges on local or regional policy making remains unclear.

Interaction with neighbour communes to reach effective scale in social infrastructure and service delivery to migrants and refugees

The neighbouring Länder Berlin and Brandenburg have a strong relationship as a common area. Plans on a fusion of the two Länder were on the political agenda repeatedly within the last decades, but lastly failed in a referendum in Brandenburg in 1996. Still, the region embarks on large common projects that create proximity and demand cooperation. For instance the innovation strategy "innoBB", that aims at establishing the region as a scientific and technological hub and ensure its economic development including in the fields of energy and health technology, logistics, transport and mobility as well as media and creative industry[1]. The close relationship is also amplified regarding issues related to migration and integration. The two Länder share a common statistical service unit (*Amt für Statstik Berlin Brandburg*) where data on i.e. migration inflows is made available for the region as a whole, as well as distinctive data for each of the Länder.

In some cases, Brandenburg and Berlin coordinated the reception of refugees and asylum seekers who were allocated by the federal level. On 8 September 2015, they agreed on making use of a common arrival train station, were refugees and asylum seekers are welcomed, supplied with nutrition and receive a medical examination before being distributed to a reception centre in the respective Land. According to the latest progress report (as of January 2016), these regulations have proven to be quite flexible[2]. In 2016 Brandenburg agreed to accommodate 1 000 asylum seekers, which had been allocated to Berlin in a reception centre at its borders to make up for shortcomings in accommodation in Berlin. This agreement was suspended in August 2017 because of lower numbers of asylum seekers arriving. Generally, the political negotiation process to achieve this regulation was quite time-consuming and complex.

2.1.2. Objective 2. Seek policy coherence in addressing the multi-dimensional needs of, and opportunities for, migrants at the local level

City vision and approach to integration

Characteristic of the state and city of Berlin is its Participation and Integration Act (PartIntG), which was the first in Germany. The Act, formulated in 2010, provides a framework defining the cross-sectoral tasks and measures. It is overseen by Berlin's Commissioner for Migration and Integration. The Commissioner heads a unit exclusively dealing with issues regarding Migration and Integration in the city. The narrative of the documents reflects the city's mentality as growing and diverse largely featuring the guiding principles of intercultural opening and equal participation of people with a migration background. (For an overview of how concepts in Berlin developed, see 2.4.4.Annex B of this study.)

The concept of intercultural opening and equal participation of the law (§4 PartIntG), addresses all administrations in Berlin, such as the departments of the Senate, all public agencies, the departments of the districts, subordinated bodies, institutions, foundations, the Parliament, audit office, and the commissioner for privacy or state-owned companies. The main aim of this paragraph is to ensure that all people, regardless of their origin have the same prerequisites and access to all services in the city. The city aims to ensure this by setting an increasing share of people with a migration background working in institutions, to better reflect the composition of Berlin's population. The municipality also addresses intercultural opening through the provision of intercultural training seminars. At the time of writing, indicators of the achievements made are being discussed. Still, a regular report on the overall process is prepared as part of the PartIntG evaluation (see the section 2.3.3 for insights on assessment).

To enhance more equal participation in Berlin's society and administration, (§ 6 PartIntG) and to encourage migrant organisations and people with a migration background to participate equally in local politics, the city formally installed the State Advisory Board on Migration and Integration (Landesbeirat für Integrations- und Migrationsfragen). It acts as a consultative body in political decision-making and is a permanent representative of people with a migration background.

Further, the law ascribes an Ombuds function (§5 PartIntG) to the commissioner for integration and migration. He or she serves as a reference person for all people with a migration background in the city and is tasked with supporting migrants and people with a migration background to enforce their rights. Citizens can express their concerns and get counselling by making an appointment during the regular counselling hours and via direct inquiry. The communities of people with a migration background are generally given the opportunity to also voice complaints through the state advisory board on migration and integration (see section 2.2.2). In this Ombuds function, the commissioner takes constant positions on migration-related political and legal topics. He or she has an explicit right to communicate and inform the public through the press, in order to draw the public's attention to the needs of people with a migration background. In this regard, the position of the Berlin commissioner enjoys substantial autonomy. Since the commissioner's office is also embedded in the administrative structure of the city's government, particularly the senate department for Integration, Labour and Social Affairs, he or she has a double-headed function. In occupying both a position within the administration of the executive power in Berlin and an ombuds function for Berlin's migrants, the commissioner has to balance between accepting and challenging political decisions made by Berlin's government. In addition to the Senate's Commissioner for Migration and Integration the §7 of PartIntG stipulates that each city district also needs to have an Integration Commissioner to represent the concerns of people with a migration background in local planning and policy design and to make proposals on how to enhance integration in the district (see the section 2.3.3 for assessment tools of the PartIntG).

In addition to this framework, the Senate drafted a cross-sectoral concept for reception and integration of asylum seekers and refugees in 2016 as a direct response to increasing inflows of this group to the city. This "Masterplan Integration and Security" constitutes a holistic framework for integration starting from day one until the individual is settled in (see the section 2.1.2). It also stresses Berlin as a city of diversity that has challenges but entails benefits. It draws on past experience and mistakes that were made in integrating migrants, while stressing the need to enable the social, cultural and occupational participation of refugees. It includes several measures that re-structure and develop the settlement process, including cooperation measures between federal and Lander levels for language training or the installation of an office for employment consultation in refugee accommodation (Berlin Municipality, 2016). Funding of the Masterplan has been implemented through scaling up existing welfare mechanisms and public services. In particular, existing projects, such as the Integration guides project (*Landesrahmenprogramm Integrationslotsinnen und Integrationslotsen* (see Objective 4) The staff of existing administrative agencies, in schools and child care and the allocation of grants for existing integration projects by third sector actors was increased. Furthermore, the Masterplan serves as a guideline for cooperation of all levels of government, the welfare system and volunteers. A monitoring report system regarding all measures has been implemented, which includes an annual report to parliament. The Masterplan is has been updated in 2018 through a comprehensive consultative process has been deployed to include the point of view of migrants, refugees and other relevant stakeholders. The new Concept for integration and participation of refugees (Gesamtkonzept Integration und Partizipation Geflüchteter) will include an evaluation mechanism focussing on indicators.

All departments take stock of integration as a cross-sectoral task and have developed policies towards migrant integration within their remit, which are usually coordinated and consulted with the office of the commissioner. For instance, the Senate Department for Urban Development and Housing implements the participatory project Soziale Stadt since 1999, which mainly focusses on urban development in particular deprived areas and also on integration of migrants in these areas, in particular newly-arrived refugees and EU-movers (for description of how these areas are identified and evaluation see the section 2.3.3).

Horizontal co-ordination infrastructure at city level

A cross-departmental topic like migrant integration challenges Berlin's complex governance structure (detailed presentation in the Box 2.1 below). Requirements for constant consultation make decisions time consuming and inhibit fast responses, yet they also ensure inclusiveness and provide limited space for issues to bypass the commissioner for migration and integration or district governments. The regular co-ordination mechanisms take place in the council of mayors, at the senate level, and in round tables or functional commissions, in lower levels, that respond to current challenges. In 2015 a co-ordination group for refugees and asylum seekers was set up. The most important co-ordination mechanism for migrant integration is the Integration-Migration conference between all district commissioners as well as senate representatives.

Box 2.1. Berlin's Governance System

In Berlin powers are divided between the legislative body, the Berliner Abgeordnetenhaus (i.e. the Berlin Parliament), which is elected by its citizens, and the Berlin Senate which heads the executive administration and is elected by the Parliament. In order to bring its principles into legislative action the Berlin Senate needs to receive the approval of the Parliament. Berlin's government is usually formed in a coalition, headed by a mayor and at the time of writing, two vice mayors. It sets the political agenda in a coalition agreement in the beginning of its legislative period and appoints functional senators. Senators have responsibility over functional departments of the senate administration – together with the mayor and vice mayors they form the Berlin Senate government.

The Senate, again, is divided in two layers. The first layer, the main administration (Hauptverwaltung) is primarily responsible for matters regarding the city and the Land Berlin as a whole. The second layer consists of the districts and is mainly operating tasks on the local level. The districts do not enjoy independent territorial authority, but are an entity of the city's administration. Tasks delegated from the main administration can be taken away at any time. Secondly, responsibilities are not clear-cut, since the main administration jointly takes over tasks concerning the local level. The upper layer is divided into 12 functional departments, which are further split into functional units. These units are headed by a senator and state-secretaries and by administrative unit managers, who both report to the department's senator. The upper level includes around 40 public agencies, which are directly subject to the functional and administrative supervision of a respective department. In their delegated scope of action however, public agencies enjoy some autonomy. Additionally, around 100 owner-operated enterprises and public institutions report indirectly to the respective functional departments, such as universities, adult education centres, hospitals or the Berlin public transportation enterprise (Berliner Verkehrsbetriebe BVG) . In general, the different competences of offices and agencies in Berlin (and Germany) follow a very complex-scheme of responsibilities and authority.

The Senate Department for Integration, Labour and Social Affairs, incorporates the unit integration, which is headed by a unit manager who is currently the Berlin Commissioner for Migration and Integration.

The 12 districts of Berlin form the lower level of the administrative structure. Their legislative organ, the parliament of each district is the Berzirksverordnetenversammlung (BVV) and the administration is called Bezirksamt, headed by a district mayor. The Bezirksamt incorporates around 10 agencies, like departments at the upper level, which have important competences in service delivery to citizens (i.e. citizens' registration office). Following the legislative framework of the PartIntG law each district is obligated to have its own Commissioner for Migration and Integration who are also active in local integration policy making.

The BVV has only limited parliamentary functions, as it does not pass laws but determines the administrative policy within the legal and administrative scope regulated by the main administration. The deputies (minimum 55) are elected at the same time as the Berlin Länder parliament. The main work of the BVV is done in committees, which are work groups consisting of deputies. Each district has a committee for Integration.

The Berlin senate government holds a formal meeting once a week. Additionally, the council of the state-secretaries (*Staatssekretärskonferenz* Stk) heading functional units, including the state-secretary for integration, meet once a week. Moreover, one-off roundtables and meetings are held when challenges and issues arise.

All matters, which have to be decided upon or have to be acknowledged by the Senate, are prepared in draft proposals, so-called Senatsvorlagen by the functional units/departments. Documents are prepared, drafted and concluded in a collaborative manner by the senate departments and passed by the Parliament. The drafts are conducted under the leadership (Federführung) of the respective Senate unit, which has the authority and functional responsibility in the area related to the issue. Moreover, one instrument of government control is written inquiries (Schriftliche Anfragen) made by parliament deputies, which are also delegated for answering to the functional responsible unit in the Senate. If certain parts of the draft's content fall under the functional responsibility of another unit, it has to be co-signed (Mitzeichnung) by the unit and thereby validate its content, make recommendations or - depending on the scope - contribute whole passages or chapters to the document. This practice has proven to be quite time-consuming and thus to some extent limits capacities. It is in particular problematic regarding the cross-sectoral responsibilities in integration policy making, since bigger projects have to be revised back-and-forth between several departments before being passed into law. However, this process is strategic for the commissioner for migration and integration in influencing draft laws/policies that are related to migrant integration issues as he or she will have to be consulted by the department in charge of the drafting process.

Through a thorough and lengthy consultative process between units (described in Box 2.1) the commissioner for integration and migration has the ability to encourage other departments to address certain issues. For instance, in 2014 the commissioner initiated and funded a research institute to conduct an 'Evaluation of Intercultural Opening of Elderly Care'. By advocating that action was urgently needed, the subject was added to the political agenda and spurred the relevant senate department (at the time: Health and Social Affairs) to take further steps.

Further co-ordination takes place through Jour Fixes, round tables and functional commissions, which are usually set up in response to current challenges. For instance, a weekly Jour Fixe regarding challenges related to Refugee Integration ("Große Lage") was initiated in 2015 as a response to high numbers of arrivals. Around 80 participants of the senate administration, districts but also representatives of welfare organisations and NGOs coordinated operative actions to establish comprehensive welcoming structures. The Berlin-wide co-ordination Unit for Refugee management (Landesweiter Koordinierungsstab Flüchtlingsmanagment, LKF), established in August 2015, was abolished in 2016 in response to decreasing numbers in inflows of asylum seekers and institutionalisation of co-ordination.

Other examples are project-based work groups, regular exchanges of districts and departments in the scope of, for instance, the Soziale Stadt project or the committee on policies for the inclusion of Roma.

Representatives of the district in particular are part of many co-ordination rounds and work groups. Their expertise and involvement is perceived to be essential, since they are oftentimes charged with implementing actions and regulations and are directly confronted with local needs. Some examples are listed below.

The council of mayors (*Rat der Bürgermeister*) is one of the most important bodies and link the upper level (*Hauptverwaltung*) to the lower level (*Bezirksverwaltung*). It meets at least once a month and is headed by the Chancellery, who convenes the mayors of the districts. Additionally, members of the Senate can participate in a consulting function. The council of mayors is a mere consultative body that recommends laws and actions for those policy sectors that are directly implemented at district level. Despite being a merely consultative organ, the council has to be involved in any substantive policy changes that the Senate wants to introduce; however, it does not have the right to appeal (Berlin.de, n.d.(a)). For instance, on integration policy, the council of mayors has a significant political impact. This was the case with the introduction of the Masterplan Integration and Security on 21 April 2016 (Bezirksamt Mitte, 2016) or with distribution of additional 'integration guides' (see the section 2.3.2) to the districts in summer 2015. In both cases, the council supported the Senate. In the case of the Masterplan the districts requested some amendments, which were taken into consideration, such as for instance a paragraph on the contribution of neighbourhood organisation programmes.

Another important venue with regards to integration is a regular co-ordination meeting among integration commissioners through the conference of the districts' integration commissioners (*Landesarbeitsgemeinschaft der bezirklichen Integrations- und Migrationsbeauftragten*, LAG). The Berlin Commissioner for Migration and Integration and staff of the Berlin Senate Unit Integration also hold regular conferences with the districts' commissioners. Since 2010, the task of the meetings is, in particular, to develop a common position on integration and migration issues in horizontal and vertical co-ordination of policies. Participation in the committee is voluntary but all districts take part.

Contribution of representatives of the districts and the LAG Integration-Migration in other Berlin- and administration-wide work groups, roundtables and committees such as participation in the Islam Forum (see the page 55 below) are conveyed by the council of mayors. One of the district mayors stated that this procedure has proven to be successful. The LAG Integration-Migration monitors to ensure that all 12 districts are represented equally among all committees in the policy area.

A challenge in co-ordination with districts is that local administrative structures of the district do not resemble those of the main administration. For instance, some stakeholders expressed that co-ordination could be simplified by establishing an administrative unit for integration in each district.

On the ground, examples in the policy area of education are so-called regional co-ordination centres. The senate department for Education, Youth and Science has introduced these centres in every district for coordinating migrant children's integration in schools (see the section 2.4.4. on Educational responses). These units act on the local level to coordinate stakeholder actions, including with the city's main administration. They consist of a member of the *Bezirksamt* and the local school boards.

2.1.3. Multi-level governance of mechanisms for the reception and integration of asylum seekers and refugees

The process from Arrival to Status Recognition

Upon arrival, asylum seekers are directed by the agency to the nearest contact point for registration. In most cases, these contact points are located close to the Länder branch offices of the BAMF. When asylum seekers register at the State Office for Refugees [Landesamt für Flüchtlingsangelegenheiten] LAF in Berlin, the LAF will decide whether the application will be processed in Berlin or in another federal state. Subsequently, asylum seekers are delegated to the nearest reception facility, in the federal Land where they are assigned. If their application is processed in Berlin asylum seekers are obliged to live in Berlin during the application process. Subsequently, information on the person is registered in a federal data system (the so-called *Ausländerzentralregister*). Asylum seekers will receive an appointment with the BAMF to file their asylum application for the first time and then for an interview. During this time the BAMF will issue a temporary residence permit as identity card.

Box 2.2. The allocation mechanism for refugees and asylum seekers in Germany

The allocation of asylum seekers and refugees is regulated in Germany through the quota system for first distribution of asylum seekers (Erstverteilung von Asylbegehrenden) called EASY in line with the so-called Königsteiner Key (Königsteiner Schlüssel). Every Land in Germany receives a percentage of asylum seekers to be allocated within its territory, which is defined every year by a federal-Länder commission. The percentage is based on tax revenue, weighted two third and population size, weighted one third. Labour market conditions are taken into account to a limited extent (OCED, 2017b; Piccinni, A. and P. Proietti, forthcoming). However, it is also taken into account which branch-office of the BAMF is responsible for handling the person's application as competence between the regional offices is divided according to country of origin. Allocation to municipalities depends on the respective Land. In the vast majority of cases, the number of asylum seekers allocated depends on the population size of the receiving municipalities. Thus, on the regional level, employment opportunities are largely not factored in (OECD, 2017b).

BAMF decides on the application based on a personal interview and initial information. Asylum seekers in Germany are classified according to asylum recognition rate of their nationality. For instance in 2017 nationalities with a recognition rate above 50% were Syria, Eritrea, Iraq, Iran and Somalia (see Annex D for statistics on German recognition rate). Depending on the nationality of the asylum seeker, different early measures packages apply. For instance federal integration courses apply for recognised refugees and asylum seekers with an above-average recognition rate (>50%) which include 100 educational units: 60 units of German classes, 40 units on cultural background. See Annex C for more details.

The BAMF chooses from four types of protection: Constitutional asylum, refugee status according to the Geneva Convention, national subsidiary protection based on EU law, rejected asylum seekers and those who are rejected but hold a

---

temporary suspension of deportation status, so called 'tolerated' (Duldung). Recognised refugees receive a permit for three years; subsidiary protection permits are valid for 1 year, both with possibility of extension.

Federal regulation foresees that recognised refugees (granted asylum, refugee status or beneficiary of subsidiary protection), have to stay within three years after registration in the area (Bundesland) they are allocated to (OECD, 2017c: 190). Refugees and asylum seekers can apply for exemption from the regulation, if they have a family member or if they found a job or educational opportunity elsewhere.

Source: OECD (2017b); OECD (2017c).

In general, Länder are obliged to provide benefits, accommodation and health services for asylum seekers and bear the full cost as regulated in 1993 in the Asylum Seekers Benefits Act (Asylbewerberleistungsgesetz). In 2016, due to a high financial pressure induced by a sharp increase in arrivals, the federal government agreed to assume part of the costs for housing and social benefits in block grants proportionately to the number of asylum seekers the Land received (OECD, 2017c; see the section 2.1.4. on funding). Berlin holds a peculiarity in centralising tasks to one agency the State Office for Refugee Affairs Landesamt für Flüchtlingsangelegenheiten (LAF), since other Länder, oftentimes delegate these obligations to municipal level. This agency, exclusively in charge of asylum seekers registration and basic sustenance. was created in August 2016 by making the Asylum area independent from the State Office for health and social affairs (Landesamt fuer Gesundheit und Soziales, LAGeSo). This decision was due to the high number of asylum seekers arrivals in 2015 that overburden the LAGeSo which was until then in charge of charge of registration, accommodation and basic sustenance for Asylum seekers on top of its tasks for providing health and social services to Berlin's general population[3]. Asylum seekers waiting in line at the LAGeSo were supported by Berliners, who brought meals and water (Tagesspiegel, 2015). To contrast the chaos created by the mountainous workload of late 2015 and early 2016 the municipality not only rebranded the LaGeSo but also introduced in October 2015 a new registration system. First-time applicants were pre-registered, accommodated and received an appointment for their registration in the shelter (IHK, 2016b). In May 2018 the LAF reception center in Berlin still received between 650 and 750 new arrivals per month for initial registration, identification and administrative proceedings4. Here they have their photos and their fingerprints digitally recorded and data that can be immediately compared to international police databases. The quota of distribution of asylum seekers in Berlin to its districts is subject to availability of accommodation.

After the applicant has registered at the public agency at the border, the closest contact point agency and potentially again at the LAF if assigned to Berlin, the person has to personally attend an appointment at the respective branch office of the BAMF before a decision on the application is made.

Once recognised, refugees receive assistance through local *Jobcentres* or Social Welfare Offices, depending on if the person is employable (*erwerbsfähig*)[5] or not. This means that refugees receive the same allocations (housing and living) as nationals. The agencies distribute social benefits, which are federal allocations. Individuals whose application is rejected are entitled to further assistance by LAF until they depart or – when the rejected person stays for more than six months – the responsibility lies with the Social Welfare Office.

There is no digital or administrative procedure in place to transfer the case of the person from all agencies responsible during the asylum seeking phase (LAF; Federal Employment Agency, etc.) to the Jobcentres. This holds also true for communication between the BAMF (in charge of the Integration courses and the asylum application approval) and LAF. Therefore, the transitory process is aggravated by the fact that the responsible agents have to redo and re-enter all administrative procedures and information. The city has addressed this issue, and a fledgling documentation system, which is voluntary, is now operational. In addition, within scope of the "early intervention" project, set up by BAMF and the Federal Employment agency, a voluntary platform for data transfer was initiated. However, it faces some constraints because of data protection laws as German data protection laws constrain access to personal data if there is no specific juridical reasons.

Accommodation for Asylum Seekers Following the German federal legislative framework, three basic types of accommodation for asylum seekers exist in Berlin: emergency accommodation and reception centres, collective/decentralised accommodation and separate facilities for the most vulnerable. Emergency accommodation and reception centres are temporary accommodations (max. six months). Asylum seekers are eligible for their own flat after six weeks of stay in a reception centre. Exceptions to this rule apply for people originating from a country with a low-recognition rate. Due to high administrative barriers and a general lack of (social) housing in Berlin, this is seldom possible. The third accommodation type includes accommodation for groups such as LGBTI, disabled, traumatised individuals or unaccompanied minors, who need separate or special treatment.

Unaccompanied minors are taken care of in dedicated centres, children's homes, child and youth living communities, youth accommodations, which are also mainly managed by NGOs and welfare organisations that provide accommodation to German adolescents. In reception centres, welfare benefits are generally disbursed as in-kind benefits.

In Berlin, the accommodation of asylum seekers has been a major concern of the city in recent years and various kinds of public venues (including schools, gymnasiums and parts of the former airport building in Tempelhof) were transformed into temporary emergency accommodation (Berlin Municipality, 2017). As of March 2018, asylum seekers were still living in temporary emergency accommodation. This is problematic as they offer limited private space and often lack infrastructure (kitchens, bathrooms etc.) to serve many people. At the same time these types of accommodation often block public space needed for recreational activities and education. Since 2017, emergency shelters with the most precarious living conditions, in particular gymnasiums have been vacated (Berlin Senate, 2017). Temporary emergency accommodation is organised by the LAF, which now primarily focuses on using prefabricated homes and containers. Apart from welfare organisations the LAF (former LAGeSo) also contracted semi-private real estate companies as operators. In the end of the year 2015 almost half of the operators were private companies as these were able to provide locations on short notice. Given the pressure of high arrival inflows, most of the operators were tendered in a short-term procedure (*Freihändige Vergabe*): foreseen for emergency situations, it allows direct contract attribution by the Senate[6]. In the aftermath, the lacking of quality checks caused problems as some operators did not provide the necessary trained staff or fulfil the basic criteria as agreed upon in the contract, such as basic health standards or the provision of a comprehensive concept for protection against violence for vulnerable groups such as women (rbb24, 2016).

In light of the gaps in accommodation standards, a debate about privatisation arose, in particular about the extent to which private companies can make a profit out of the accommodation of asylum seekers (Zeit Online, 2015). As a reaction to these shortcomings, the Senate established a quality-check work group in the LAF and the tendering process was adjusted to ensure quality requirements are monitored. In particular the Berlin State Office for Equal Treatment and Against Discrimination, (Landesstelle für Gleichbehandlung - gegen Diskriminierung) LADS enacted several measures in assisting LGBTI refugees.

Moreover, in a session on 7 February 2017 the Senate decided to establish a state-owned operator to complement the welfare organisations and NGOs in accommodating asylum seekers and applicants, focused on a similar model implemented in Hamburg. Representatives of the project in Hamburg assisted in the design, which was under the responsibility of the senate department for Finances, LAF and the state-owned real-estate-management company Berliner Immobilienmanagement GmbH. On 19 April 2017, the state-owned operator took over the first emergency facility. As of 2017 Berlin, Hamburg and North-Rhine Westphalia were the only *Länder* that still run emergency accommodations (. They persisted because there were still not enough joint facilities available. Also already earlier in 2016 the Berlin senate decided to create the state-owned construction company *BEFU*, which plans to create 8 000 additional units before 2019. These units will then be lent to the LAF. The state owns 51% of the cooperation, while the already established private construction company Berlinovo owns 49% (Berlin Senate, 2016).

Asylum seekers and refugees are encouraged to look for private housing. Asylum seekers who would like to live in their own apartment can apply for a Rent take-over certificate ([Mietübernahmeschein) issued by the Municipality[7]. This certificate states the size and maximum amount of the rent that will be taken over by the LaGeSo. After the asylum procedure an entitlement to housing benefits may exist through the *Jobcenters,* as part of the social welfare programme like other people in need. In interviews with the OECD, some stakeholders said that looking for private accommodation is a major challenge for refugees who often lack the needed networks and language skills.

Specifically, beneficiaries of the subsidiary protection status, who hold a 12-month residence permit, generally find it challenging to move out of collective housing facilities. Some welfare organisations (such as the Evangelical Youth and Welfare organisation) are tasked by the municipality to advice beneficiaries of the take-over certificate, who can only sign the rental agreement after their advice[8]. In order to avoid homelessness, it is possible to stay in collective accommodation also after recognition. The rationale for this decision is the tight housing market, which is likely to get worse in coming years (Berlin Senate, 2017). In the meantime, the city has built so-called "tempohomes", temporary state-owned lightweight housing with a limited lifespan. In order to avoid segregation and exclusion, recent facilities are spread across the city.

Labour Market Regulations

Economic conditions in Germany, including civil society's firm commitment to immigration and a robust job market that is comparatively open to integration (although safeguards exists), enhances the likelihood that asylum seekers and refugees will integrate German society quickly (OECD, 2017b: 11).

Box 2.3. German Integration Act (2016)

In August 2016, a new Integration Act came into force that simplifies early integration of asylum seekers into the labour market. It introduces three major changes in access to the labour market for asylum seekers and refugees (OECD, 2017b: 190).

First, for denied asylum seekers and those holding *Duldung* status, the so-called 3+2 rule was introduced. The rule entails that under certain conditions, denied asylum seekers and tolerated persons are guaranteed a *Duldung* for the duration of an apprenticeship (three years) and if they subsequently find a job within six months after completion, they are handed a residence permit for an additional two years of work experience (OECD, 2017b: 12, 46; OECD, 2017c: 190). The German apprenticeship includes practical experience in a company, enterprise, or public body and a theoretical component (vocational education in a school) (OECD, 2017b: 13). Local municipalities play a crucial role in facilitating networks between job-seeking asylum seekers and refugees and local employers (see Box 2.7)

A second novelty introduced with the Integration Law, was a suspension of the so-called priority verification (Vorrangprüfung) for three years in 133 of the 156 districts of the Federal Employment Agency. The regulation entailed that asylum seekers were only allowed to take up a certain position if no other person holding a residence permit had applied for the job. Thus, residence permit holders, naturalised and native-born individuals were given priority by the regulation. It was however inappropriate for persons holding higher education credentials or had high-skilled qualifications in professions with a general national shortage in the workforce.

A third novelty was the federal government initiation of special measures to further facilitate the integration of asylum seekers and refugees into the German labour market, so-called "Refugee Integration Measures" (*Flüchtlingsintegrationsmaßnahmen*, FIM). All asylum seekers are eligible to take up certain collective tasks while benefitting from accommodation and catering, i.e. maintenance of public gardens and receive allowances. The municipality distributes these federal means (EUR 0.80 per hour of work) through the club or association where asylum seekers perform the community service. The aim is to encourage first work experiences and to strengthen mutual cultural understanding as well as language learning of participants. This measure was significantly reduced in 2017 and most of its funding redirected due to a lack of demand. *Source:* OECD (2017b); OECD (2017c).

Asylum seekers can request a permission to work after three months from filing their application. The permission will be issued by the Aliens' authority [Ausländerbehörde] who will involve the Federal Job Agency [Bundesagentur für Arbeit] in this process. The permission to work during the asylum procedure only refers to a specific offer of work that the applicant has received. However Asylum seekers are not permitted to perform a self-employed activity[9].

The Land of Berlin is currently developing a concept for active labour market integration for asylum seekers and refugees. The concept is expected to be part of the comprehensive Framework for Integration, which will aim to enhance participation of refugees and asylum seekers in the city. The aim is to link offers and actors and thereby establish a common support structure. This also includes the further development of minimal quality standards of counselling and support offers. The concept follows up on a draft proposal of the Berlin Senate (*Senatsvorlage*) regarding "additional measures for the Integration of refugees and asylum seekers in apprenticeships and work in 2015", as well as on the Masterplan Integration and Security (see the section 2.4.1 for Measures regarding labour market integration of migrants).

2.1.4. Objective 3. Ensure access to, and effective use of, financial resources that are adapted to local responsibilities for migrant integration

The municipal departments and districts share funding for integration measures based on the principle of non-interference, authority and responsibility. The draft of the budget law is conducted by the Senate Department of Finance in cooperation with all other departments.

The budget law of the state of Berlin currently encompasses revenues and spending of around EUR 25 billion in 2016/2017. A big, but declining, share of the budget is traditionally spent on debt and interest payments. In accordance with the financial responsibilities and obligations in the federal-state scheme, most of the budget is allocated to education, with an average of EUR 5 billion (2015, 2016, 2017 around 20% of the budget) and social services with, on average, EUR 4 billion (2015, 2016, 2017 around 15%). Another example of shared responsibilities across the districts is the way in which the budget is distributed. The main administration is entitled to around 68% of the budget (2014 and 2017 roughly EUR 16.5 billion), while districts receive about 32% (2014 and 2017 around EUR 7.7 billion). The remaining is distributed to judiciary bodies. Almost half of the budget (EUR 3.9 billion) of the districts is spent on social services.

The Senate administration for Labour Integration and Women received EUR 183 million in 2017 (i.e. 0.7% of the overall budget). Almost 50% of the department's budget is spent on Labour Affairs and vocational training. The share of the budget allocated to the Commissioner for migration and integration in the senate department increased from 2014/2015 (EUR 11 million) to 2016/2017 (EUR 18 million) from around 6.6% to 10 % (department share). The *Integrationguides* (see section 2.2.1) are one example of a project that is fully covered by the Commissioner. In 2016, funding was increased especially to districts that host more refugees such as Mitte. Funding in 2014 amounted in total to EUR 2.2 million; 2015 to EUR 2.2 million; 2016 to EUR 4.4 million and in 2017 to EUR 4.5 million.

The relatively small budget of the commissioner does not represent all financial resources spent on integration in the city state. First, integration, as explained above, is considered a cross-cutting policy. Thus, many measures of other senate administrations are funded out of budgets of other units and departments. Secondly, federal entities such as BMI, BMAS, the Federal Commissioner for Migration and Refugees and the Federal Ministry for Family Affairs, Senior Citizens, Women and Youth (BMFSFJ) provide earmarked funding for integration measures at the local level. Further, the EU provides earmarked funding through AMIF, EHAP, EFRE and ESF. EU funding is usually distributed by the city and is subject to EU regulations. Since many different stakeholders are involved in integration policy making (including NGOs and welfare organisations, districts and nearly all administrative entities and sub-ordinated agencies), it is very challenging to estimate shares and amounts of financial flows to migrant integration from all levels to the local one.

For instance integration efforts in districts are in general funded through different sources, they result from the implementation of wider projects such as Soziale Stadt, the Roma Action Plan or Integrationguides, as well as integration-targeted federal projects and measures (i.e. BAMF).

The Social City or *Soziale Stadt*, described in detail on page 38,) is jointly financed by EFRE (EU), the federal government and the Berlin government. See Table 2.1 for an overview of Soziale Stadt, which is a good example of a shared funding mechanism.

Table 2.1. Funding Overview: Project Social City (*Soziale Stadt*)

	EFRE (European Union)	Federal Level	Berlin
Action and Project Funding	0 %	33.3%	66.7%
Construction Funding	50%	16.7%	33.4%
Network Funding	50%	0%	50%
Area-Teams	25%	25%	50%

Financial Flows for asylum seekers and refugees

As stated above, Länder are in general obliged to fully cover costs for basic sustenance for asylum seekers and those who have been declined residence permits by BAMF. However, due to high financial pressure from rising numbers of asylum seekers, the federal government agreed to provide block grants for accommodation and social benefits in 2016 (amounting to EUR 8 billion until 2018 for the 16 Länder) (OECD, 2017c). Länder receive an additional lump sum of EUR 670 per asylum seeker. An agreement was reached after a rather fierce negotiating period[10]. According to latest estimation, Germany spent a total of EUR 16 billion (0.5% of GDP) on asylum seekers and refugees in the year 2015 alone (OECD, 2017c).

For the Masterplan Integration and Security, the Senate agreed to spend another EUR 41 million for special integration offers (new funds to support guardianships, schooling in welcome classes and mentoring).

Berlin provided in the scope of the Masterplan EUR 16 million and in 2017 and EUR 12 million for neighbourhood projects in districts through a district integration fund that districts can spend themselves. The districts also receive funding, from the Länder administration, for additional staff costs for the integration of refugees and asylum seekers.

Box 2.4. Block 1 Key Observations

- The city of Berlin enjoys substantial room of manoeuvre with regard to migrant integration polices, due to its dual role as both city and Land. For example, it is responsible for education, spatial planning and local economic development and thus benefits from access to important co-ordination mechanisms that take place at both the Länder and city level (e.g. 'Conference of Ministers for Integration of the Länder', and the 'Communal Quality Circle Integration'.

- The National Action Plan for Integration represented an attempt to co-ordinate integration policymaking involving Länder, cities and towns. Some stakeholders argue that Berlin's first integration concepts served as a role model in the development of a first federal National Integration Plan in 2007. Contributions of the different government levels would still benefit from better co-ordination.

- Specific to Berlin is its Participation and Integration Act (PartIntG), which was the first one of its kind in Germany. Among other things, the law regulates equal access to services and ensures equal participation in local politics. In addition, the so-called 'Integration and Security Masterplan' from 2016 and updated in 2018 is a cross-sectoral vision for asylum seeker and refugee reception and integration.

- Integration mechanisms are institutionalised through a Commissioner for Migration and Integration who oversees all city-wide integration work and acts as an Ombudsman. In addition, each district also has a Commissioner for Migration and Integration. Still, the cross-departmental nature of local integration polices challenges Berlin's complex governance structure. The large amount of consultations, due to its state character in the German system, makes decisions very time-consuming and often delays responses.

- The city reacted quickly to the peak of refugee and asylum seeker arrivals between 2015-2016. In Germany the Land are responsible for asylum seekers registration, reception and sustenance therefore Berlin had to quickly adapt existing structures to the increase demand. On the one hand, the city quickly formulated a response strategy in 2016, the so-called 'Integration and Security Masterplan' updated in 2018, on the other, it separated the asylum area of the State office for Health and Social affairs creating the self-standing State Office for Refugee Affairs (*Landesamt für Flüchtlingsangelegenheiten*) LAF. This State body centralises all the responsibilities of the Land in terms of asylum seekers reception.

2.2. Block 2 Time and space: Keys for migrants and host communities to live together

Across the ten cities analysed in the case studies, the concepts of time and space appear to be essential in conceptualising sustainable solutions. Time is understood as the continuum in which solutions are executed in the city: from short-term reception and orientation, to long-term settling in the city along the key milestones of a migrant and his/her family lives. Space is understood as proximity. Different communities can connect around spaces, activities, causes or housing solutions that facilitate regular interaction and break down prejudices and cultural barriers.

It is becoming more and more evident that acquiring a host country's language and social norms as early as possible is essential to increase a migrant's or refugee's chances to find employment (OECD, 2017b). However, these skills are essential not only to newcomers, but also to other groups who might have been in the city for longer but have failed to acquire them.

2.2.1. Objective 4. Design integration policies that take time into account throughout migrants' lifetimes and status evolution

Measures that take time into account

The city of Berlin aims to provide a support structure from "moment zero" of arrival to settling in. This is especially visible in its recent Integration and Security Masterplan and other measures developed recently.

The Masterplan is laid out as a holistic framework and takes into account needs at different stages from arrival to recognition of status and beyond in addressing issues related to asylum seekers' reception, housing, education, childcare, health care, job consulting, language courses and participation. Examples of early intervention initiatives include "Integration Packages for refugees", a brochure available in English, French, Arabic, Farsi/Persian[11] which contains information to provide initial orientation, as well as vouchers for Language and Integration courses and an offer for an education consultation. Further, 'Welcome in Work' (*Willkommen in Arbeit*) and 'Integration' offices are available in large reception centres. These offices channel different types of offers in a single contact point and are conveniently located within housing facilities for refugees and asylum seekers.

In 2016, the "Welcome Centre" (*Willkommenszentrum)* was established to offer counselling to all newcomers on the services at their disposal as well as legal and administrative issues regarding immigration and integration. The services are available to all migrants regardless of their reasons for entry, even though since 2015 the Senate identified refugees explicitly as a target group. Just like any other newcomer, refugees and asylum seekers can turn to the Welcome Centre for a first-orientation consultation on questions regarding their stay, health insurance system, school education, tax system, vocational training opportunities, as well as job search.

To complement federal regulations that only provide language courses to those asylum seekers originating from a country which have a high asylum recognition rate (>50%)[12] , the city provides courses for all other applicants. These are financed by the city and take place in one of 12 adult education centres. Since adult education centres are part of the city of Berlin, implementation does not necessitate supplementary contracting.

Furthermore, the federal government and the city offer specific courses for vulnerable groups such as women with children and LGBTI.Courses serve as an important contact point to reach out to the target group. Many offers in Berlin, such as the mobile education counselling service (MoBiBe, see chapter 2.4.1) reach newcomers directly at this venue. Other organisations offer insight into topics such as participation, democracy, human rights and fundamental freedoms, workers' rights and vocational training on the 'dual apprenticeship system'.

While the most recent migrant integration mechanisms primarily target early integration aspects, there are also offers geared to migrants who have been living in the city for a substantial period of time. In 2013, Berlin established the "Integration-guides" programme *(Landesrahmenprogramm Integrationslotsinnen/Integrationslotsen)*, which engages people with a migration background to accompany newly-arrived migrants, but also individuals who have resided in the city for a longer time and require support. They provide translation and intercultural mediation services. For instance, guides accompany families and individuals to appointments in the city's registration offices or in the process of school enrolment as well guidance in finding work. Guides do not have to have specialised educational credentials before participating but receive training. The commissioner's office for migration and integration coordinates the project and allocates annual funding to districts for the guides. Contracted NGOs and welfare organisations implement the project on the local level. The success of the project can be found in the ease with which migrants can access its services, as implementation takes place at the district level. About 50 000 individuals have accessed these services during the last three years. The project, which has been established as a best practice, has been replicated by other municipalities throughout Germany.

Stadtteilmütter (neighbourhood mothers) is another long-standing programme that started in 2004, enabling integration oriented social work also on the local level. During a 6-month training programme, unemployed women with a migration background are trained to council other families of their communities on various subjects, such as health, education and parenting. The neighbourhood mothers cooperate with local institutions such as schools, kindergartens, parent and neighbourhood meet-ups and local counselling units for youth. In this way, they spread their knowledge, make use of their language and cultural skills, and receive a qualification as a social assistant as well as a two-year job contract. While the project has many positive advantages, such as providing unemployed women with a job and giving them recognition for what they do, it also reproduces very traditional "care-taker" roles for women, confining their expertise to the private realms, instead of also encouraging a more equal distribution of roles between men and women (Schreiber, 2011). In 2017 around 920 Stadtteilmütter were qualified through the programme, most of them in Neukölln (420), Kreuzberg (180) and Mitte (320). In Neukölln alone, around 10 000 families were visited.

2.2.2. Objective 5. Create inclusive urban development policies that prevent the physical and social isolation of people with a migrant background

As mentioned in section 1.2, Berlin aims to highlight cultural diversity as part of its "brand", which suggests that diversity is a notion that is generally accepted in Berlin's society[13].

Cultural facilities in Berlin are an important venue for exchange between people with and without a migration background. Berlin's cultural institutions ensure that their offers are open to a multilingual audience. For instance, more than 60% of the cultural institutions use multilingual material for their public relations material. While some offerings address people merely as consumers, others have a participatory nature. Funding for cultural projects (e.g. the *Participatory Arts Projects*) by the Berlin Senate is often subject to specific conditions such as diversity-specific goals. Many cultural institutions are also offering free entrance to refugees and asylum seekers. The Senate Department for Culture has also implemented a project "be Berlin – be diverse" in order to raise awareness of this topic.

The programme 'Soziale Stadt', a federal wide project implemented in Berlin, is a participatory programme to stabilise and upgrade neighbourhoods that are disadvantaged from a social, economic and urban planning perspective. The approach aims to create social cohesion and foster interaction in designated areas and neighbourhoods in Berlin. This is done by combining social local festivities and events are organised such as neighbourhood walks and intercultural picnics, street fairs and fast-breaking with changes in the urban infrastructure, making spaces more attractive to rest, play and exercise by increasing the open spaces and vegetation. Participating venues aim in particular at intercultural exchanges through inclusion of all groups residing in the area and include local stakeholders. A central factor for the success of the project is the participation across departments in the local administration and the facilitation of a participation culture for local residents. Each neighbourhood is equipped with an office and a neighbourhood management team that functions as a focal point. The programme is part of federal-Lander cooperation and mutually funds similar projects all over Germany and is also supported by the European Regional Development Fund (Quartiersmanagement Berlin, 2016). Neighbourhood councils function as an advocacy group for the residents and decide how funds will be used.

One project funded by the budget of Soziale Stadt is "BENN", Berlin develops new Neighbourhoods (Berlin Entwickelt Neue Nachbarschaften). BENN implements inclusive urban development initiatives in areas close to big reception centres for newly arrived asylum seekers and refugees in cooperation with the respective district and local stakeholders. The participatory action plan seeks to strengthen community ties in for instance the establishment of a neighbourhood forum to engage all inhabitants in a dialogue and encourages grassroots neighbourhood forums and roundtables in the areas and districts (Stadt Berlin, n.d.).

The Senate Unit for Education indicated that schools also play an important role in fostering community between people with and without a migration background in the city. Offers are built on inclusion and interaction between all groups of children but also between their parents. Meet-ups in school festivities provide important venues in this regard. In particular, in schools with a high share of migrant children many offers for exchange and inclusion of parents are provided, usually jointly with local NGOs, social workers and welfare organisations. The involvement and commitment of the school (see the section 2.4.4. on educational responses) is the biggest factor determining the success of such events. Best practices in this regard, identified by the unit, are Parent-Cafés (Elterncafés) or so-called Parents Seminars (Elternseminare), which also include, for instance, educational sessions for parents on raising kids in a bilingual environment for instance Turkish and German.

Apart from these official structures there is a variety of volunteer initiatives and projects for intercultural exchange. One big, well-known project is the Workshop of Cultures (Kulturwerkstadt) that functions as a cultural meeting and event location embodying the slogan: 'We celebrate cultural difference'. It is located on the former grounds of the

Wissmannstraße Brewery in Berlin-Neukölln. In 2017, it had 45 000 visitors holding up to 50 events per month ranging from film screenings, panel discussions, and theatre, dance and music festivals that deal with topics like migration, intercultural identities, diversity and equal opportunities. Its most popular event, which was created in 1996, is the 'Carnival of Cultures', an annual open-air festival, held in summer, attracting 1.5 million visitors to Berlin every year celebrating the city's cultural diversity. This project is implemented by the association "Brewery Wissmannstreet" (Brauerei Wissmannstrasse e.v.) and several other associations and partners.

Another successful example is the social start-up Migration Hub Network. Following the heightened societal interest in the issue of migration integration, the initiative set out to better structure this emerging societal interest in the subject of migration and to connect projects. Headquartered in Berlin, the global network aims to increase information exchange between grassroots projects and foster collaboration between social entrepreneurs, foundations, investors and government organisations to facilitate innovative solutions regarding mass migration. The hub provides a common open co-working space for initiatives that deal with migration and integration issues. This presents an important opportunity especially for grassroots and 'newcomer' organisations to evolve, since they often lack financial means, access to research, networks and data. It also benefits established initiatives, corporations, academia and other private actors active in Corporate Social Responsibility (CSR) in an exchange of best practices. The network is recognised as a "Landmark in the Land of Ideas" (Deutschland Land der Ideen) by the Federal Government and the Federation of German Industries and was awarded the Shimon Peres Prize by the German-Israeli Future Forum and the German Ministry of Foreign Affairs for its exchange between Berlin- and Tel Aviv-based activists and social entrepreneurs.

Consultative mechanisms to ensure the participation of migrants and refugees

In Berlin, consultation with citizens and possibilities for citizens' participation exist at the state, district and neighbourhood level.

In the scope of the 'Soziale Stadt' programme described above, all citizens residing in a certain area can become part of a neighbourhood-council and define local urban development. In this way, citizens' concerns as well as suggestions are taken into account. In addition, the BENN projects established a resident council (Bewohnerrat) for asylum seekers and refugees residing in bigger residential buildings in Berlin. The venue aims at identifying needs for action to improve living conditions and development of the accommodation as well as to discuss possibilities for involvement of the respective group in local communities.

On the districts' parliamentary level (BVV), all citizens can, under certain conditions, participate, consult and vote in meetings as so-called citizen deputies (*Bürgerdeputierte*) (see the page 15.) Further, all BVVs have an integration work group or committee. Regulations (§ 9 BezVG) stipulate that participation is set at a minimum of four citizens. Like the BVVs, the committees do not have the right to draft legislation; however they may develop recommendations. The city does not gather data on how many citizen deputies are migrants or have a migration background, so the participation of the target group in committees cannot be estimated.

Involvement of migrant organisations in Berlin's integration policy is ensured through consultation mechanisms, notably the State Advisory Board on Migration and Integration (*Landesbeirat für Integrations- und Migrationsfragen*). Since 2010, the Board has a legal status in Berlin, as defined in § 6 PartIntG. It meets four times per year under the leadership of the senator for Integration, Labour, and Social affairs. The Advisory Board has agenda-setting powers. Its main task is developing recommendations, which are later submitted to the Senate and stakeholder-associations. Second, the State Advisory Board on Migration and Integration has to approve the appointment of Berlin commissioners for migration and integration. This further emphasises his/her Ombudsfunction as a representative for the migrant community. The board is comprised of seven representatives from migrant associations including one repatriate organisation (*Aussiedler*), several city and district officials and several representatives of civil society. The representatives from migrant associations are elected in a public meeting by registered migrant organisations. The following persons and entities are also members: the state-secretary for integration, the commissioner for migration and integration, a representative from the council of the districts, a representative of the commissioner for migration and integration of the districts, and representatives of third sector associations including the Berlin Refugee Council.

Another consultative organ, which should be mentioned in this context, is the Islamic Forum of Berlin (*Islamforum Berlin),* which has become since 2005 the most important co-ordination committee between the Muslim community and the government in Berlin. It is an initiative of the Berlin commissioner for migration and integration and the *Muslimische Akadamie* (Muslim Academy) and takes usually place four times a year. The agenda is determined in cooperation with the Muslim community shortly beforehand and usually addresses current issues and events. Since the Islamic Forum is not a legally institutionalised forum, the Senate is not entitled to give mandates or assignments to the Islamic Forum. Thus, its scope of political influence lies in directly influencing participating members (of the different departments of the Senate) and in raising awareness of certain topics on the agenda, which are, as mentioned above, set jointly with the community itself.

While sessions are not open to the public, they not only include representatives of Islamic organisations and civil society but also representatives of the major religious communities such as the Jewish, Catholic and Protestant community. Further, they include the city representatives of the Berlin Senate, notably the Interior senator and the mayors of the districts and other units depending on the subject to be. A study on prevention of violence and radicalisation assigned by the European Commission (Change Institute, 2008) emphasised the Islamic Forum as a 'best practice', as it engages stakeholders of the political sphere, Muslim organisations and civil society actors in a genuine dialogue around a broad set of activites.

Box 2.5. Block 2 Key Observations

- Berlin's more recently adapted mechanisms demonstrate the importance to start integration of migrants as early as possible. Especially with regard to refugee integration the development of "Integration Packages" as well as "Welcome to work" centres demonstrate this understanding. They channel different offers through a single contact point shortening administrative waiting times. Further, complementing federal offers, integration courses are also made available to asylum seekers with less than (>50%) recognition rate to ensure fast integration.

- Leveraging the knowledge of migrants who have been living in Berlin for a longer period. The city provides them with training sessions that enable them to draw on their own experience to act as a Guide and support newly-arrived migrants to get acclimated to their new city

- To upgrade disadvantaged neighbourhoods, many of which have large migrant populations, the city adopts local programmes to foster integration and to create social cohesion. This is done by combining local festivities and events, such as neighbourhood walks and intercultural street fairs, and by adapting the urban infrastructure. This includes making spaces more attractive to rest play and exercise by increasing open spaces and vegetation. Further, a large variety of small volunteer initiatives and projects for intercultural exchange that serve as meeting places for migrant and non-migrant populations can be found in the city. Examples are the Workshop of Cultures (Kulturwerkstadt) and the Migration Hub Network.

2.3. Block 3 Capacity for policy formulation and implementation

2.3.1. Objective 6. Build capacity of public services, with a view to ensuring access to mainstream services for migrants and newcomers

Developing public servants' intercultural and diversity skills and ensuring equal treatment in the recruitment of public servants

The city of Berlin has stipulated the equal participation and the process of intercultural openness in the PartIntG law (see the section 2.1.2.), demanding all institutions within its jurisdiction to ensure both. All institutions must ensure advanced training in intercultural competences for their employees and consider this a relevant skill in recruiting. One example of implementation is provided by Berlin's biggest public hospital Charité, which has taken part in a model approach for intercultural openness. The project included mainly so-called diversity seminars, for both the management level and other staff.

Further, the Berlin Senate aims to increase the share of staff with a migration background in institutions so that it is equal to the share of people without a migration background. Developments are monitored based on a set of indicators and have to be reported back to the legislative political body, i.e. the city's parliament. Further, all public job postings must mention that candidates with a migration background are encouraged to apply (GVBI. 2010: 560).

The city of Berlin is aware of the value of experience sharing with other subnational governments to increase local capacities thus it engages in many peer learning activities. Berlin exchanges on challenges and best practices through a network of 17 partner cities[14] called City Partnership[15], including Brussels, Budapest, Buenos Aires, Istanbul, Jakarta, London, Los Angeles, Madrid, Mexico City, Moscow, Paris, Beijing, Prague, Tashkent, Tokyo, Warsaw and Windhoek. Additional cooperation exists in certain related policy areas through, for instance, European associations of subnational governments (e.g. Eurocities).

The Membership of Berlin in the German Day of Cities mentioned on section 2.1.1 also systematically enhances the experience sharing about measures regarding immigration, integration and refugees. Measures include a regularly held conference on integration in cities as well as website features publishing practical examples of integration on the local level from each of its member cities and the publication of reports, the most recent one discusses refugee integration, listing challenges and solutions at the local level (Deutscher Städtetag, 2016).

Additionally, the Integration Department of Berlin is also a member of the 'Communal Quality Circle Integration' (Kommunaler Qualitaetszirkel zur Inetgrationspolitik), which facilitates the exchange of best practices on integration among local commissioners for integration as well as research institutions, foundations and the BMBF. The goal of the circle is to support municipalities to develop a monitoring mechanism based on indicators measuring integration outcomes (Stuttgart, n.d.). Berlin is also a member of the Municipal Association for Administration Management (Kommunale Gemeinschaftsstelle fuer Verwaltungsmanagment, KGSt). This association, in collaboration with two large German foundations (Bertelsmann Stiftung and Robert Bosch Stiftung), recently published a report on communal integration management providing concrete examples for administrative setup for the co-ordination of measures and offers for integration within municipalities and with external partners (KGSt, 2017).

2.3.2. Objective 7. Strengthen co-operation with non-state stakeholders, including through transparent and effective contracts

Non-commercial and charitable third sector service providers continue to play a very active role in the area of integration in Germany and Berlin. They act as important service providers and are incorporated into the federal social policy framework (Schmid/Mansour, 2007: 244). In line with the concept of subsidiarity, many social services are outsourced to highly professional local associations, NGOs or neighbourhood organisations and volunteers (Bendel, 2014: 5). These are organised in huge umbrella organisations to represent their interest and offer advice on the federal and Länder level (Schmid/Mansour 2007: 244). Their activities are limited to the delivery of charitable-, non-commercial- and/or church-related tasks (Schmid/Mansour 2007: 244). Six German branches of welfare umbrella organisations (*Spitzenverbände der freien Wohlfahrtspflege*)[16] and subordinated incorporated associations on the local level are integrated in public policy making and receive funding form implementing social policies. Self-organised (local) organisations need to become part of the six umbrella organisations in order to benefit from their influence and means. Also the local organisations/associations are highly professionalised and well-staffed (Bendel, 2014: 5). In addition, foundations are important donors and policy advisors to federal and local governments through their research work as well as chamber of commerce and trade unions. This study thus includes an analysis of how the city of Berlin cooperates with, includes- and contracts third sector entities in their integration policy scheme.

Civil Society Engagement

In response to the increased numbers of asylum seekers and refugees in Berlin a huge wave of solidarity from civil society could be witnessed. During the summer of 2015 many volunteers spontaneously helped out in temporary sustenance and emergency relief. This included the collecting and distributing of donations (e.g. clothing and food), providing translation assistance as well as arranging accommodation in their own homes where the public system was overburdened. Initiatives, projects and social start-ups dealing with more long-term social and economic integration issues emerged engaging to provide services such as language training and job matching. While some of these initiatives professionalised over time and are still existent others disappeared with declining numbers of refugee and asylum seekers arriving in the city.

The city adapted to this new situation by explicitly valuing and acknowledging the civil society and volunteer engagement. It has included the empowerment and co-ordination with volunteers and neighbourhood organisations in the Masterplan Integration and Security, which aims to formalise a 'culture of acknowledgment' for voluntary work and help structure work processes and information sharing with and amongst initiatives.

For instance, the city provides an online platform (www.berlin.de/buergeraktiv or www.berlin.de/fluechtlinge/berlin-engagiert-sich), listing all social initiatives for people who are looking to get involved. It also provides initiatives with practical information on association and volunteer management including insurance and legal requirements. As volunteer work on asylum and refugee aspects often requires in-depth knowledge of administrative systems and legal regulation the city cooperates with large NGOs and also offers qualification courses that provide information on intercultural communication and support in dealing with particularly vulnerable groups.

Further, in all large hosting facilities for asylum seekers and refugees the Senate engaged coordinators for volunteer work, who organise the activities in the facilities and cooperate with local stakeholders and the Senate administration. The LAF has organised a monthly exchange with all volunteer actors, including the coordinators in accommodation and representatives of the Network *Berlin Hilft* (Berlin Helps). All districts have organised their own volunteer and mentoring networks, some are organised around larger housing facilities, some with a focus on specific areas. As mentioned in section 2.1.4., the district received additional grants for supporting neighbourhood initiatives (EUR 9.2. million in 2017) as outlined in the Masterplan.

Outsourcing and Grants

Social services - including those for migrants, asylum seekers and refugees in Berlin - are mainly outsourced to welfare organisations and NGOs in line with the German tradition of subsidiarity described above. As also observed in Vienna and Amsterdam, outsourcing is a main component of Berlin's way of implementing integration policy and does not only complement services. Hence, the mandate to carry out important services is often delegated to welfare organisations or NGOs (i.e. in sustaining civil society initiatives, implementing Integration Guides, etc.).

Depending on the service tendered, Berlin relies on welfare organisations and NGOs but also the chamber of commerce, neighbourhood organisations, foundations as well as associations and migrant organisations. All must fulfil certain tendering criteria, which means many welfare organisations must provide highly professional services. Distinction and consideration of the different types of entities in the Berlin context in carrying out services is relevant in their scale of implementation. While (smaller) entities are mainly operating on the local (district) level, other larger, more professionalised ones are often active Berlin-wide. Tendering processes are usually implemented via public bidding and follow institutionalised rules, which are set in a legal framework. When contract values exceeds a certain threshold, processes of public bidding fall under European public bidding law and have to be tendered on the EU platform TED/ECAS to comply with non-discrimination clauses.

As per the budget law of the Senate, which is renegotiated every two years, contracts for integration services usually have the same length. This bears the risk of service discontinuity and exposes service providers and their employees to uncertainty when it comes to funding. Multi-year funding plans could increase the financial stability and sustainability of projects. Some contractors hired by the municipality stated during interviews with the OECD, that they focus their work mainly on the short-term, since their services, especially regarding asylum seekers, do not receive long-term funding.

Besides outsourcing, the municipality as well as foundations provide grants empowering various stakeholders such as NGOs and migrant associations. Empowerment of migrant associations through the provision of grants is a central tenet of the city's strategy (see the section 2.1.2). The Participation and Integration Agenda (*Partizipations- und Integrationsprogramm*) is one example through which the city funds projects. Each year the commissioner's office provides grants for around 35 initiatives (budget in 2014/2015: EUR 1.526 million; 2016/2017 around EUR 2 million).

As outsourcing and the provision of grants is a common practice and exists in various forms, some are given rather more autonomy in the implementation, while others are more controlled in objectives and specific targets. Meaning also that monitoring mechanisms are diversified and experiences vary widely among senate administrations. Some service providers have to reach distinct benchmarks, such as the project integration guides where providers have to fulfil distinct criteria. Grants for local projects are provided in a selection procedure by the respective senate department. In the *Zuwendungsdatenbank* (funding/grant database) introduced in December 2010, all grants activated by the Senate and the district departments are listed. In 2015, 8 582 projects were financially supported by the state as a whole; 202 of these projects are labelled to concern the policy area of integration (Berlin.de, n.d.(b)). It is not further specified however, what the criteria of this label entails. In addition, the city introduced a transparency database in 2011 where beneficiaries should voluntarily indicate their expenses. The ones introducing extended information are rewarded in receiving a quality label, the "transparency emblem"[17] (Senate administration for Education, Youth and Science, 2012). In 2017, 7 955 organisations were listed, while 1 613 carry the transparency emblem. (Berlin.de, n.d.(c)).

2.3.3. Objective 8. Intensify the assessment of integration results for migrants and host communities and their use in policy design

For a quantitative evaluation of the state of integration of people with a migration background, the Berlin Commissioner's office for migration and integration makes use of the Integration monitoring system of the Lander, which offers a variety of indicators and has also been used to conduct information for this study. The monitoring tool is in particular valuable since it provides common and comparable indicators across Länder and is conducted throughout the federal state by all Länder. A general obstacle in assessment abilities and thus co-ordination of activities, as expressed by some stakeholders in Berlin, is that the definition of the target group, people with migration background, varies in conception and statistical data collection across levels of government and institutions.

The overall integration strategy, the PartIntG law, is evaluated biannually by the Berlin commissioner's office for migration and integration. The office is committed to reporting the state of the law's implementation to Berlin's parliament. However, there is no enforcement mechanism in place whereby the results of the report have to be taken into account in the next policy making cycle. As of the time this paper was published, three evaluation reports were conducted, in October 2012, June 2015 and October 2017. Evaluations have a qualitative nature and are based on surveys among public servants in the Senate, as well as in the districts of Berlin. Monitoring of intercultural openness is the main component of the assessment. Specific goals connected to the strategy are listed and inform intercultural training programmes and responses by the departments and stakeholders listed. Other fields of actions include intercultural competences in job profiles, as well as for promotions. In addition, outcomes and work of the State Advisory Board on Migration and Integration are listed.

To collect qualitative results, Senate departments and districts have to answer a set of questions mainly related to measures taken regarding the state of internal processes of intercultural openness. However, as mentioned above, the assessment does not include a users' survey interrogating people with a migration background for instance about their access to certain services. It was stated in the 2012 evaluation report that an inquiry of private stakeholders and institutions would go beyond its possible scope (Berliner Abgeordnetenhaus, 2012: 2). The second and third evaluation report also included, apart from reports from all senate departments and districts, reporting from 39 (partly) state-owned Berlin companies (e.g. the public transportation company *Verkehrsverbund Berlin-Brandenburg GmbH*).

Further evaluations of integration programmes are conducted independently and usually follow the same pattern (i.e. participative biannual inquiry, and presented to the Parliament). The evaluations of local integration programmes and projects are often outsourced to expert groups and consultant offices, such as the evaluation of Integration Guides, which was commissioned to the research institute Camino gGmbH in 2015 (Kahn-Zvorničanin et al., 2015), and reports on the Roma Action Plan (*Aktionsplan Roma*). The aim of expertise outsourcing is to get an objective external assessment of the project's performance.

In addition, the Office of the Berlin Commissioner for Migration and Integration refers to existing research, conducted by foundations, the chamber of commerce and research institutions. The office also encourages research in contracting research institutions, such as in 2014 for an expertise on cultural diversity in schools and the intercultural openness of the administration regarding discrimination in Berlin to the think tank SVR[18] or the above-mentioned study on Intercultural Opening in elderly care.

The Senate introduced a new concept for the integration of refugees in 2017. As a basis, the senate department is planning to contract an expert research agency for an evaluation of the current state of refugee integration in the city. The report will focus on the amelioration of interlinkages between the Berlin Senate (*Länder* level) and the districts as well as with volunteer activities. In addition, the development of spatial planning in districts, equal access to the offers in the areas of education, labour, accommodation, health and local infrastructure as well as the participation of migrants and refugees in empowerment for self-organisation and public discourses in general are to be addressed in the report. The implementation of the strategy, based on preliminary findings, is to be further guided by the expertise of this external consultancy.

The department of culture has initiated an audience development initiative called KULMON (since 2011) to evaluate cultural diversity in Berlin's cultural institutions and is currently expanding their evaluation on how people with a migration background make use of cultural facilities in the city and thereby take part in the various activities the city offers.

The Senate Department for Urban Development and Housing has been monitoring socially-deprived and segregated areas through the monitoring tool Soziale Stadtentwicklung (Social Urban Development) since 1998. Since disparities exist within districts, monitoring and policy development focuses on so-called Sozialraumorientierung (social area orientation). The comprehensive framework identifies areas within districts through indicators such as long-term unemployment rates and child poverty rates (Berlin Senate, 2015: 11). Apart from other local socio-demographic premises, the tool monitors the share of migration background and foreign born population in distinct areas and identifies links between certain socio-demographic settlements and deprivation, while identifying distinct potential. The monitoring serves as an early-warning system and groundwork for action and development for urban development policies in certain areas.

Box 2.6. Block 3 Key Observations

- According to its Integration and Participation Act all of Berlins' institutions must ensure advanced training in intercultural competences for their employees and consider this a relevant skill in recruiting. Developments are monitored and have to be reported back to the legislative political entity, i.e. the city's parliament.

- The traditionally large body of non-commercial and charitable third sector service providers are very active in the field of integration in Germany and Berlin. In line with the concept of subsidiarity, many social services are outsourced to highly professionalised local associations, NGOs or neighbourhood organisations and volunteers. Subject to the budget law of the Senate, which is negotiated every two years, some contracts for integration services bear the risk of service discontinuity and exposes service providers and their employees to uncertainty when it comes to funding. To provide transparency on expenditures, the city has a funding/grant database (Zuwendungsdatenbank) that lists all grants disbursed by the Senate and the district departments.

- Integration outcomes of Berlin are captured in the Integration monitoring tool of the Länder, which offers a variety of indicators and provides common and comparable indicators across Länder. It is a regional evaluation taking place under a coherent template led by the Länder North-Rhine-Westphalia and Berlin. The overall integration strategy, the PartIntG law, is evaluated biannually by the Berlin commissioner's office for migration and integration. However, there is no enforcement mechanism in place for the results to be incorporated into the implementation of future policies.

2.4. Block 4 Sectoral policies related to integration

2.4.1. Objective 9. Match migrant skills with economic and job opportunities

With the introduction of the new integration law in July 2016 access for refugees and asylum seekers was further facilitated.

In Berlin the full-time employment rate for people with migration background is 20% lower than for native-born and 10% lower than the national average. The participation of people with a migration background in apprenticeships is particularly low at only 4-5% (Berlin Municipality, 2017). In the multi-level governance scheme of the federal republic, labour market integration is not a responsibility of municipalities. However, in light of city-specific challenges such as the particularly high gap between people with and without a migration background regarding employment and apprenticeship participation, the city makes specific efforts to unlock the potential of people with a migration background for the local labour market.

This is particularly important given the increasing labour market prosperity and the lowest levels of unemployment since reunification; the jobs created in private companies and public service often target a high-skilled and well-trained labour force that possesses a high level of German language skills. Often qualification levels among migrants, asylum seekers and refugees, do not fulfil these requirements. For around one-fourth of those who declared themselves as seeking work, data on educational attainment is missing. Consequently, the Senate Unit for Labour concluded that 59% of this group are only able to be placed in assistant and low-skilled jobs (Senate Unit for Labour, 2017). Further, people with a migration background also often have lower chances to benefit from the new jobs created, as they obtain weaker educational results than their native peers, have a higher unemployment rate and participate less in apprenticeships. According to the city, sectors such as production, building, services, security and transport and logistics are those that offer most potential of employment for low qualified people in Berlin (Berlin Municipality, 2017).

In order to better match migrants' skills with local labour market needs Berlin focuses early interventions on assessing skills as well as on support for recognition of certificates and credentials obtained abroad, connected with need-based educational training (Interview, Senate Unit for Labour Affairs). There is a clear need for intensive support measures for migrants, refugees and asylum seekers to be placed in qualification programmes such as apprenticeships and work. Obtaining an apprenticeship has proven to reduce risks of future unemployment and enables the participant to receive a general higher income (Senate Unit for Labour, 2017). One of the projects implemented is *Berlin needs you!* (*Berlin braucht dich!*), initiated in 2006. The aim is to increase the percentage of people with a migration background in dual-apprenticeships by focusing on transition mechanisms. The first component of the project creates links between businesses and schools through establishing encounters starting at a young age and repeatedly until graduation. The project is based on collaboration with 70 partnership organisations, most of which are (partly) state-owned (such as hospitals, Berlin water supply, fire brigades, police or public transportation). Second, it engaged public actors and civil service providers (such as the police, fire brigade). Third, it contacted 15 private companies in the metal and electricity industry. The participation of the third group was negotiated by German trade union associations (*Deutscher Gewerkschaftsbund* DGB). The second component of the project is consulting partnership organisations on changing their recruitment process and communication.

The Berlin committee for vocational training (*Landesausschuss für Berufsbildung*, LAB) also concerns itself with the integration of refugees in apprenticeships and work. The committee consists of the department of Integration, Labour and Social Affairs; Department for Education, Youth and Family; Department for Economics, Energy and Enterprises, representatives of employers' organisations (chambers of commerce, company officials, associations, etc.) as well as representatives on the employee side with the participation of members of trade unions. The aim of the LAB is to match employers and employees in order to cope with rising demand for skilled labour and helping the local population (and the labour/apprenticeship market) perceive people with a migration background as a potential gain for the community. The LAB facilitates exchanges between different stakeholders in setting integration of people with a migration background into the Berlin labour market as a common goal and task.

For an assessment of newcomer abilities, the Senate funds the Berlin educational counselling service of the *Berliner Bildungsberatung MoBiBe* (Berlin mobile education counselling service). MoBiBe's multi-lingual counselling targets the individual's potential in referring them to suitable offers within the educational system, vocational training or the labour market. The specific value of the programme lies in the inter-linkage to other services and in easy access due to its mobile character. The consulting centres of MoBiBe are spread out through the city, while some consultants work directly in reception centres in so-called Welcome-to-Work offices. MoBiBe was able to adjust quickly to changes in accommodation situations and demands. In this way, early intervention could be ensured. Moreover, MoBiBe is connected to offers of all adult education centres (*Volkshochschulen VHS*) in the city, where people are introduced to their offers in integration and language courses. This further lowers the barrier to take advantage of the counselling.

An initial assessment of asylum seeker and refugee skills is conducted in Welcome-to-Work offices. The offices are located in reception centres and larger refugee housing facilities. The offices pool all educational and labour services offered in Berlin such as counselling on labour market prospects, apprenticeships and education as well as legal rights and financing. They collaborate with neighbourhood organisations such as the Integration Guides who accompany refugees for administrative appointments and are also present in the centres. Similar services are also offered in the Welcome Centre in Berlin (see section 2.2.1.), regardless of the title of residence the person holds.

Berlin itself is not responsible for the recognition of qualification obtained abroad. This is the responsibility of the state and federal level. The Federal Ministry for Labour and Social Affairs (*Bundesministerium für Arbeits und Soziales*) funds the IQ network (Network Integration through qualification) for counselling and information regarding the recognition process. In addition, as recognition can be expensive, the federal and local government offer additional financial means in this regard for migrants who fulfil certain conditions (Federal level: Recognition Fund, Anerkennungszuschuss, Land Berlin: Fund for hardship cases Recognition Berlin, "Härtefallfonds Anerkennung Berlin")[19]. To make regulations more transparent for employers, the job qualification verification law *Berufsqualifikationsfeststellungsgesetz* (BQFG) and its complementary Berlin counterpart (BQFG Berlin) serve as reference.

Box 2.7. Linking Refugees to Local Employers

Several Projects in Berlin aim at creating better connections between employers and potential employees.

The Local South Berlin branch office of the Federal Employment Agency has central competencies for asylum seekers and set up a team called "Asylum Seekers". Jointly with specialised teams in Berlin Jobcenters, it establishes information events and job fairs to facilitate the first contact between applicants and companies.

An especially practical oriented approach is the educational training and labour market initiative ARRIVO. The project links migrants and asylum seekers with Berlin's businesses and employers in 'practice workshops', provides job-related language support, in addition to skills assessment in companies and placements. The success of the project is largely due to its close cooperation and linkage with private business, employers and other local stakeholders. ARRIVO gathers the many isolated measures by companies and other stakeholders, which address asylum seekers and refugees in the city, and points the applicant to a suitable offer. According to the Berlin Senate Labour unit, five sub-projects exist (as of April 2018), which cover the areas of crafts, the hospitality industry, construction, health and social industry as well as technical areas All projects share the same aim: to assist refugees in their orientation and integration in the Berlin labour market. An important aspect of the project is the ability to offer as much practical experience for refugees as possible, ideally in form of internships. Networks are thus created between applicants and employers seeking labour are established. In April 2018, more than 200 companies were engaged in the network Berlin-wide, which offer internships, qualifications and apprenticeships. In addition, an ARRIVO service office opened in August 2016. The service offers counselling for companies, on matters such as the legal status of refugees and asylum seekers, recognition of qualifications and counselling on different sub-project areas.

The project 'bridge – network for a right of residence', counsels and offers skill assessment for migrants and refugees regarding the different residence permits. The commissioner for Integration and Migration collaborates with eight NGOs that intervene to find a suitable job in co-ordination with the JobCenter, employers and businesses. Through finding employment, apprenticeships or internships the projects aims at permanently securing residence permissions. Half of the financial means are provided by the European Union (ESF-fund), 40% from the federal Ministry for Work and Social Affairs and 10% from municipal budget.

This initiative also tried to reach out to the private sector through communication campaigns. In 2017 for instance a series of billboards was produced with the slogan "Refugee is not a job".

The potential of entrepreneurial spirit of the community of all people with a migration background in the city is a distinct particularity of Berlin. According to the Senate Department for Labour, many migrants have been self-employed in their country of origin before coming to Berlin: the rate of self-employed with a migration background is higher (20.5% of the working population with a migration background) than for people without (15%) and exceeds the federal average (10.1%) by far (Berlin Municipality, 2017). For one, this denotes a distinct potential of the group. On the other hand, due to the structural disadvantages (education, discrimination, etc.) people with a migration background face on the Berlin labour market, the high numbers can be also interpreted as a compensation strategy in not being able to engage in other types of employment. However, Berlin has successfully established a network of support and advice to migrants seeking self-employment or wanting to start their own business. One example is the regular meet-up of relevant institutions and representatives of migrant communities to discuss issues of self-employment and entrepreneurship of people with a migration background. Start-up seminars in cooperation with migrant communities were established in 2003. Furthermore, issues of migrant entrepreneurship are featured regularly at Berlins' annual entrepreneurship event DerGUT (German Start-up and Entrepreneurship Day.).

Companies in Berlin and Germany are engaged in integration of people with a migration background including asylum seekers and refugees through various means. For them the Berlin Partner for Economy and Technology GmbH (Berlin Partner fuer Wirtschaft und Technologie) is an important partner facilitating this work. For instance the Berlin *Business Immigration Service* that was established in partnership with the Chamber of Industry and Commerce (IHK) aims at supporting local businesses in recruitment and legal access to labour market credentials especially for skilled work-force from outside Germany. Further the Matching Platform "alle-helfen-jetzt.de" was initiated by the enterprise Berlin Partner for Economics and Technology GmbH. The aim of the platform is to connect job-seekers with employers. Employers and companies, which are engaged in helping unlock the potential of people with a migration background can get an overview of existing projects to be supported. The platform is supported and financed by many companies and their networks, such as visit Berlin, Association of Employers in Berlin and Brandenburg (UVB), Association of German Hospitality and Eestaurants (*Deutsche Hotel- und Gaststättenverband*, DEHOGA). Furthermore, some German and Berlin companies and enterprises gather in the network "Wir zusammen" (We together) to channel integration offerings and initiatives such as measures for qualification, orientation and social engagement.

2.4.2. Objective 10. Secure access to adequate housing

While being praised for the low rents and affordable housing just a few decades ago, the housing market in Berlin is becoming increasingly tight. In particular, social housing is limited.

Pursuant to federal law, access to social housing is generally granted through *Wohnberechtigungsschein*, a social housing permit for citizens who have an income below a certain threshold and have a residence permit for at least 11 months. The permit is issued by agencies in the districts (Berlin.de, n.d.(d)). Statistics indicate that people with a migration background experience worse housing conditions than nationals. The personal living space for families with children under 18 is, on average, 7.7m² smaller for people with a migration background than for people without a migration background (Integrationsmonitoring der Länder, 2017). Berlin's main approach to improve the housing situation is to increase the social housing stock (OECD, Questionnaire, 2017). From 2016 onwards Berlin receives EUR 31.5 million per year from the federal government to support social housing. The average volume for social housing building has been increased from 1 000 apartments in 2015 to 3 000 in 2016 annually. For the new legislative period, a further gradual increase to 5 000 apartments is planned. The current plan is to extend the programme by an additional 500 apartments each year until the number of 5 000 sponsored apartments is reached. Subsidies are provided to developers who build new housing projects anywhere in the city. These apartments can only be let to low income households with a limited rent.

2.4.3. Objective 11. Provide social welfare measures that are aligned with migrant inclusion

In Germany all types of social welfare for all groups are financed through taxes. Benefits are not conditional to having worked before or having paid taxes in the country. The only prerequisite is lack of resources at their disposal to secure their living by themselves. Migrants (including asylum seekers and refugees) are thus entitled to receive assistance. However, different types of benefits exist; for migrant groups, residence title is the most important criterion determining which social scheme they are entitled to. Ensuring equal access to existing welfare mechanisms, such as public services and hospitals, is an important national priority and also features in the city's creed: 'intercultural openness'. Newly arrived still face structural barriers. Many public authorities only provide information, forms and applications in German. Moreover, the complex system of shared responsibilities between public agencies is often difficult to understand for outsiders.

As a general rule all people holding a valid residence permit have access to the German health care system through the statutory public health insurance (*gesetzliche Krankenversicherung*), which is built on a public solidarity model. The German health care system is partly subsidised by the federal government, thus tax-based, but mainly financed from contributions of its members (employers and employees). Those entitled to any kind of welfare benefits, as well as children and retirees in Germany (and thus unable to pay contributions) also receive basic health care and are exempt from membership fees.

Migrants are entitled to welfare benefits, depending on residence status. Asylum seekers are entitled to healthcare pursuant to the asylum seekers benefits act. In general this refers to the treatment of illnesses including all respective provisions, medication, and vaccinations. In Berlin, asylum seekers receive an electronic "health card" upon their arrival that allows them to visit a doctor whenever necessary. Where accommodation exceeds 500 persons, so called med-points are in place that provide basic health care through general practitioners.

After recognition, health care for asylum seekers is equal to that of other recipients of social benefits. As soon as asylum is granted, Jobcenters or Social Welfare Offices grant access to health insurance.

Regarding psychological support, asylum seekers are informed and interviewed by social workers in accordance with EU-directive 2013/33/EU right after arrival in an institutionalised medical check-up (usually in reception centres) to ensure that vulnerabilities are identified as soon as possible. Identification of especially vulnerable categories is still possible after this first assessment through volunteer workers, counselling, etc. In 2008, Berlin created a network for vulnerable categories, which coordinates the work of seven non-state welfare organisations and NGOs who provide further assistance. These organisations also have a mandate for issuing credentials for vulnerability (including: LGBTI, unaccompanied minors, disabled, pregnant women or traumatised individuals).

If necessary, asylum seekers receive psychological support or treatment. Authorities address special needs whenever possible, such as the choice of accommodation, to the extent allowed by the overall situation and availability of locations. The city's welfare system is not yet fully equipped to meet the demand of psychological assistance to the target group of refugees. The Berlin University of Medicine (Charité) and its psychiatric services initiated the project 'Central psychiatric assessment point' (*Zentrale psychiatrische Clearingstelle, ZPS*). Asylum seekers with mental health needs receive a diagnosis by a mental health professional (supported by an interpreter) and short-term help. For further treatment and therapy, ZPS refers patients to other psychiatric hospitals or office-based psychiatrists.

Since there is no federal health policy in place regarding undocumented migrants, the city refers to services provided for people without insurance by NGOs. For instance, *Malteser Migranten Medizin* (an NGO) is a medical point that provides services to people who do not have health insurance.

2.4.4. Objective 12. Establish education responses to address segregation and provide equitable paths to professional growth

Education is a competence of the Länder in Germany. In Berlin, the Senate Department of Education, Youth and Science is responsible for all matters concerning education for both municipal and federal state. Berlin's education law requires schools to provide a place also to minors who do not have a residence title in Berlin. In addition the Berlin school law obliges schools to enforce diversity and inclusion of all groups (§§ 1. 3 and 4 Berlin School Law). Districts, in particular the respective district authority (*Bezirksamt),* provide school places and organise the schooling facilities (i.e. equipment).

The Senate department of Education, Youth and Science has elaborated several means to support integration of migrant pupils in Berlin. Representatives of the Education Unit have specifically identified language barriers as an obstacle for integration of migrants in the education system. In addition cultural and psychological problems such as traumatisation can hamper the process.

In general, schools and districts enjoy freedom in design and implementation. Due to the fact that all children attend schools close to their residence the share of asylum seekers, refugees and migrants varies from school to school and is often higher in disadvantaged neighbourhoods. Hence, the implementation of concepts and approaches, such as engagement in parent support structures, diverge throughout schools in the city. Representatives of districts and local stakeholders indicated that the ability of schools to design concepts is a good practice, as it makes it possible to respond to these individual challenges.

The main component of the department's strategy are so-called welcome classes (*Willkommensklassen*), which were initially introduced with the Roma-Action plan in 2011. Their aim is primarily to enable children of migrants, newly arrived, including asylum seekers and refugees to attend and switch into regular classes as soon as possible. Classes exist at all schooling levels and affiliated in all school types. In the lowest elementary level, which corresponds to the first and second year of primary school, students should be integrated into regular classes right away. Some schools introduce welcome classes at this level[20]. Welcome classes also exist in vocational schools and upper secondary schools (*Oberstufenzentren*). Starting in 2014, a concept was further developed and modified. In particular, new arrivals during 2015 and 2016 accelerated this process. Until 2014, not enough teachers were allocated and classes had a mere temporary character. Since then, the city has developed an optional training course for teachers of welcome classes. Regulations now foresee that children spend 6-12 months in a welcome class, depending on the individual situation (i.e. language level, literacy). Many stakeholders in Berlin's education system stated that from their experience it is more sustainable to give children time, than to count on fast transitions. Others, however, criticised the concept and operation of welcome classes as fostering segregation and argue for more inclusive concepts. Whereas the aim is to include participants of such classes from the beginning at least partly in regular schooling, practice has shown that in many schools the welcome classes (both teachers and students) fail to integrate into the regular classes. Schools with a sustainable concept for integration and capacities in their regular classes tend to offer smooth integration processes to the newly arrived children and adolescents. The Senate Unit Education has further established so-called "Bridge Courses" that give students further language support in their period of transition from the welcome classes into the regular school system.

Schools, which establish welcome classes, receive general funding for additional teacher positions and expenditures from the Berlin Senate. The number of welcome classes has increased significantly from 120 in November 2012, to 317 in December 2014, 639 in December 2015 to 1,054 in December 2016. Since then the number has been somewhat stable with 1 051 in July 2017. Welcome classes amount to approx. EUR 60 million in additional staff costs[21]. Due to the recent increases, many new concepts and approaches have been tested in recent years. Some have proven to be successful, while others have already been eliminated. The Senate Unit for Education is currently developing updated guidelines for all welcome classes. However, delays have been reported to take into account recent changes and adapt to trial and error of emerging approaches.

The Senate Unit for Education identified local regional co-ordination centres as a best practice to coordinate actions. The centres are tasked with quality checks, evaluation of individual transition possibilities to regular classes as well as placement of newcomers through an initial testing, the so-called *Sprachstandsfeststellung* (language level determination and evaluation of prior knowledge).

In addition, to manage the increasing number of incoming students that bring diverse linguistic, cultural, religious, educational and other backgrounds Berlin has established a plan that provides a general curriculum, as well as a basic and compulsory framework guiding schools with the integration of newcomers, covering school education from first to tenth grade, which will come into effect by the school year of 2017/18. The new curriculum includes, for example, language promotion in all subjects and intercultural education as a central cornerstone. To further facilitate mutual understanding, intercultural education has become compulsory in the newly-developed school curriculum.

The BISS programme - Education through Language and Writing (*Bildung durch Sprache und Schrift*) - is a joint Federal-Länder initiative, which also engages Berlin schools in their work in Welcome classes. It aims to connect the content of regular school subjects to language training, which has been identified as a best practice by some schools.

Civil society initiatives also represent very interesting opportunities for migrants, refugees and asylum seekers to advance in their education. Voluntary initiatives, particularly at the beginning of the increase in inflow of asylum seekers at the end of 2015, have been a big support to manage the organisation of school education for a rapidly increasing student population in Berlin. For example, volunteers help at schools, participate in lessons in welcome classes, and provide help with translations. According to the Senate Unit of Education, volunteers make a major contribution to service provision. One of many examples is "Kiron higher education", an organisation dedicated to the education of refugees. It is committed to supporting refugees worldwide, giving them the opportunity to graduate with an accredited university degree and limit the human potential that is wasted through the lack of recognition of foreign diplomas. Kiron was founded as a start-up in Berlin in 2015 and has their headquarters as well as some classes in Berlin.

From June 2016 until September 2019, the Berlin Chamber of Commerce and Industry together with participating Berliner companies will provide funding to integrate young refugees and asylum seekers in Berlin. The aim is to promote the academic success, societal and economic integration of this group. The funded project supports 250 refugees (scholarships) in participating in its digital study programme in combination with professional mentoring and language courses.

Box 2.8. Block 4 Key Observations

- Education is a competence of the Länder. In Berlin, the Senate Department of Education, Youth and Science is responsible for all matters concerning education for both municipal and federal state. Welcome classes are an important component of the department's strategy to integrate migrants, asylum seekers and refugees into Berlin's regular schooling system. As of 2017/18, Berlin had established a plan that provides a general curriculum, as well as a basic and compulsory framework, guiding the way in which schools welcome migrants.

- Asylum seekers and refugees in Berlin receive an electronic "health card" that allows them to use the medical system. As soon as asylum is granted, refugees are thus granted access to regular health insurance.

- These socio-demographic structures show that there is a need for intensive support measures for migrants, refugees and asylum seekers to be placed in qualification programmes such as apprenticeships and work. The project "Berlin needs you!" (Berlin braucht dich!) aims to increase the percentage of people with a migration background in dual-apprenticeships by focusing on transition mechanisms. It sets up important networks between businesses and recent graduates and consults businesses on adapting their recruitment process and communication to attract people with a migration background.

- For an assessment of newcomer abilities, the Senate funds the Berlin educational counselling service of the Berlin mobile education counselling service (Berliner Bidungsberatung MoBiBe). MoBiBe's multi-lingual counselling aims to unlock individuals' potential by referring them to suitable offers within the education system, vocational training or the labour market. The added value of the programme lies in the inter-linkage to other services and in easy access due to its mobile nature.

- The potential of entrepreneurial spirit of the community of all people with a migration background in the city is a distinct particularity of Berlin. The

---

> rate of self-employed with a migration background is higher (20.5% of working population with a migration background) than for people without (15%) and exceeds the federal average by far. This points to the group's latent potential, but could also indicate structural disadvantages in accessing the regular labour market.

Notes

[1] Der Senat von Berlin (12. Januar 2016): Fortschrittsbericht über die Zusammenarbeit zwischen den Ländern Brandenburg und Berlin sowie die weitere Zusammenlegung von Behörden und Sonderbehörden.

[2] Der Senat von Berlin (12. Januar 2016): Fortschrittsbericht über die Zusammenarbeit zwischen den Ländern Brandenburg und Berlin sowie die weitere Zusammenlegung von Behörden und Sonderbehörden.

[3] See: https://www.berlin.de/laf/ueber-uns/pressemitteilungen/2017/pressemitteilung.615821.php.

[4] See: https://www.dw.com/en/berlin-refugee-authorities-keen-to-show-off-germanys-improved-asylum-process/a-43829605.

[5] Erwerbsfähigkeit is a term from German Social Law. The term includes all people who could be able to find employment. A person does not belong to this group in case of long-term sickness or disability, which keeps them from being able to work for longer than three hours per day.

[6] VOL/A § 3 section 1 p. 3.

7 www.berlin.de/ba-treptow.../pdf/information_package_for_refugees_englisch.pdf

[8] The welfare organisation Evangelisches Jugend und Vorsorgewerk EJF Berlin Moabit. From 2014-2016 it made placements to 4 700 apartments. During that time period the staff of the organisation doubled from 9-18. EJF Jahresbericht p. 356-359; www.ejf.de/fileadmin/user_upload/aktuelle-pdf/2016/Jahresbericht_EJF_2015_web.pdf.

[9] www.berlin.de/ba-treptow.../pdf/information_package_for_refugees_englisch.pdf.

[10] While Länder claimed that only 40% of costs were covered by the federal government, the federal government claimed that it amounted to up to 70%.

[11] www.berlin.de/ba-treptow.../pdf/information_package_for_refugees_englisch.pdf.

[12] At the time of writing people originating from Syria, Eritrea, Iraq, Iran and Somalia.

[13] Interview Berlin commissioner for migration and integration 8 March 2017.

[14] Berlin has formalised city-to-city agreements with these cities. These are made to internationalise Berlin's economy, science and cultural sector and foster cooperation on a subnational level.

[15] https://www.berlin.de/rbmskzl/politik/internationales/staedtepartnerschaften/

[16] The six organisations are: Arbeiterwohlfahrt, Caritasverband, Diakonisches Werk, Paritätische Wohlfahrstverband, Deutsches Rotes Kreuz, Zentralwohlfahrtsstelle der Juden. (Schmid/Mansour 2007: 244).

[17] Senate Administration for Education, Youth and Science Merkblatt zur Transparenzdatenbank (as of July, 3 2012)

[18] German title: Kulturelle Vielfalt in der Schule, interkulturelle Öffnung der Verwaltung und Diskriminierungseinschätzungen in Berlin – Sonderauswertung des Forschungsbereichs beim Sachverständigenrat deutscher Stiftungen für Integration und Migration (SVR) anhand von Daten des SVR Integrationsbarometers 2014.

[19] See: www.anerkennung-in-deutschland.de/html/de/berufliche_anerkennung.php

[20] Following the guidelines for welcome classes this should happen only in a few exceptional cases where primary schools introduce welcome classes as a response to waves of newcomers. In these cases, schools have to develop a holistic language training concept.

[21] Information obtained from the Senate Unit for Education and Masterplan Integration and Security 2016.

References

BAMF (2016), *Asylgeschäftsstastik*, www.bamf.de/SharedDocs/Anlagen/DE/Downloads/Infothek/Statistik/Asyl/201612-statistik-anlage-asyl-geschaeftsbericht.pdf?__blob=publicationFile.

Bendel, P. (2014), *Coordinating Immigrant Integration in Germany. Mainstreaming at the federal and local levels*, Migration Policy Institute Europe, Brussels, www.migrationpolicy.org/sites/default/files/publications/Mainstreaming-Germany-FINALWEB.pdf.

Berlin Municipality (2017), *Answers to OECD questionnaires for the case study.*

Berlin Municipality (2016), *Masterplan Integration und Sicherheit Entwurf,* www.berlin.de/rbmskzl/aktuelles/politik-aktuell/2016/meldung.458963.php.

Berlin Municipality (2014), *Broschüre Berlin - Eine Erfolgsgeschichte - Zahlen. Daten. Fakten.*, www.berlin.de/rbmskzl/_assets/publikationen/broschuere_berlinerfolgsgeschichte_dez14_bf.pdf.

Berlin Senate - Department for Integration, Labour- and Social Affairs (2017), "Ziel erreicht - alle Turnhallen sind wieder frei", *Press Release,* www.berlin.de/sen/ias/presse/pressemitteilungen/2017/pressemitteilung.578519.php.

Berlin Senate - Departmenent for Finances Berlin (2016), "Neue Landesgesellschaft für Neubau von Flüchtlingsunterkünften gegründet", *Press Release,* www.berlin.de/sen/finanzen/presse/pressemitteilungen/pressemitteilung.490447.php.

Berlin Senate (2015), *Monitoring Soziale Stadtenwicklung,* www.stadtentwicklung.berlin.de/planen/basisdaten_stadtentwicklung/monitoring/download/2015/MonitoringSozialeStadtentwicklung2015.pdf.

Berlin Senate (2005), *Vielfalt fördern - Zusammenhalt stärken Integrationspolitik für Berlin,* www.via-bund.de/integrations-konzepte-landesebene/berlin/Integrationskonzept_fuer_Berlin.pdf.

Berlin.de (n.d.(a)) "Politik in Berlin", www.berlin.de/politische-bildung/politikportal/politik-in-berlin/, (accessed April 2017).

Berlin.de (n.d.(b)), "Zuwendungsdatenbank", www.berlin.de/sen/finanzen/service/zuwendungsdatenbank/, (accessed April 2017).

Berlin.de (n.d.(c)), "Organisationen suchen – Transparenz", www.berlin.de/buergeraktiv/informieren/transparenz/transparenzdatenbank/index.cfm?dateiname=organisation_suche_transparenz.cfm&anwender_id=5, (accessed April 2017).

Berlin.de (n.d.(d)), "Service Wohnberechtigungsschein Antragstellung", https://service.berlin.de/dienstleistung/120671/, (accessed April 2017).

Berliner Abgeordnetenhaus (2012), *Bericht zur Umsetzung des Gesetzes zur Regelung von Partizipation und Integration in Berlin (PartIntG) sowie der übrigen Bestimmungen des Gesetzes zur Regelung von Partizipation und Integration in Berlin.*

Berliner Morgenpost (2016), "In Berlin wurden 11.000 Asylanträge zu viel gestellt", *Berliner Morgenpost,* www.morgenpost.de/berlin/article206939037/In-Berlin-wurden-11-000-Asylantraege-zu-viel-gestellt.html.

Bezirksamt Mitte (2016), "Rat der Bürgermeister unterstützt den Masterplan Integration und Sicherheit des Senat", *Press Release,* www.berlin.de/ba-mitte/aktuelles/pressemitteilungen/2016/pressemitteilung.470506.php.

Boulant, J., M. Brezzi and P. Veneri (2016), "Income levels and inequality in metropolitan areas: A comparative approach in OECD countries"

Bundesregierung (2007), *Nationaler Integrations Plan*,
www.kmk.org/fileadmin/Dateien/pdf/Bildung/AllgBildung/2007-10-18-nationaler-integrationsplan.pdf.

Change Institute (2008), *Study on the best practices in cooperation between authorities and civil society with a view to the prevention and response to violent radicalisation*,
www.changeinstitute.co.uk/images/publications/changeinstitute_preventingradicalisation.pdf.

Charbit, C. (2011), "Governance of public policies in decentralised contexts: The multi-level approach", *OECD Regional Development Working Papers*, No. 2011/04, OECD Publishing, Paris,
http://dx.doi.org/10.1787/5kg883pkxkhc-en.

Charbit, C. and M. Michalun (2009), "Mind the gaps: Managing Mutual Dependence in Relations among Levels of Government", *OECD Working Papers on Public Governance*, No. 14, OECD Publishing, Paris. doi:10.1787/221253707200

Deutscher Städtetag (2016), *Flüchtlinge vor Ort in die Gesellschaft integrieren: Anforderungen fuer Kommunen und Loesungsansaetze*, Deutscher Städtetag, Berlin and Köln,
www.staedtetag.de/imperia/md/content/dst/veroeffentlichungen/beitraege_stadtpolitik/betraege_zur_s tadtpolitik_109_integrationsbroschuere.pdf.

Federal Commisioner for Migration, Refugees and Integration (2016), *Bericht der Beauftragten der Bundesreigerung für Migration, Flüchtlinge und Integration - Teilhabe, Chancengleichheit und Rechtsentwicklung in der Einwanderungsgesellschaft Deutschland*,
https://m.bundesregierung.de/Content/Infomaterial/BPA/IB/11-Lagebericht_09-12-2016.pdf;jsessionid=319EAF33171B32B6D42B30DBA0466463.s2t1?__blob=publicationFile&v=6.

Federal Office for Migration and Refugees (2016), *Migration, Integration, Asylum Political Developments in Germany 2015: Annual Policy Report by the German National Contact Point for the European Migration Network (EMN)*,
www.bamf.de/SharedDocs/Anlagen/EN/Publikationen/EMN/Politikberichte/emn-politikbericht-2015-germany.pdf?__blob=publicationFile.

Federal Office for Migration and Refugees (2005), *The Impact of Immigration on Germany's Society: The German Contribution to the Pilot Research Study "The Impact of Immigration on Europe's Societies" within the framework of the European Migration Network (EMN)*,
www.bamf.de/SharedDocs/Anlagen/EN/Publikationen/Forschungsberichte/fb01-einfluss-zuwanderung.pdf?__blob=publicationFile.

Gesemann, F. (2006), "Grundlinien und aktuelle Herausforderungen der Berliner Integrationspolitik", in *Politische Steuerung von Integrationsprozessen: Intentionen und Wirkungen*, VS Verlag für Sozialwissenschaften, Wiesbaden, 195-213, https://doi.org/10.1007/978-3-531-90454-2_9.

Gesemann, F. (2001), *Migration und Inetgration in Berlin. Wissenschaftliche Analysen und politische Perspektiven*. VS Verlag für Sozialwissenschaften, Wiesbaden

Gesemann, F. and R. Roth (2015), *Integration ist (auch) Ländersache! Schritte zur politischen Inklusion von Migrantinnen und Migranten in den Bundesländern*, Friedrich-Ebert-Stiftung, Berlin,
http://library.fes.de/pdf-files/dialog/11197.pdf.

GVBI [Gesetz- und Verordnungsblatt fuer Berlin] (2010), *Gesetz zur Regelung von Partizipation und Integration in Berlin*, P. 560, 66. Jahrgang, Nr. 32, Senatsverwaltung fuer Justiz.

Höhne, J., B. Linden, E. Seils, A. Wiebel (2014), *Die Gastarbeiter: Geschichte und aktuelle soziale Lage*, Hans-Böckler-Stiftung, Düsseldorf, www.boeckler.de/pdf/p_wsi_report_16_2014.pdf.

Hübschmann, Z. (2015), *Migrant Integration Programs: The Case of Germany*, The Global Migration Research Paper Series, Global Migration Centre (GMC), Geneva,
http://repository.graduateinstitute.ch/record/292694/files/GMPRS_N11_2015.pdf.

IHK (Industrie und Handelskammer) Berlin (2016a), *Berliner Wirtschaft in Zahlen*, www.businesslocationcenter.de/imperia/md/blc/wirtschaftsstandort/standort/content/berliner_wirtscha ft_in_zahlen.pdf.

IHK Berlin (2016b), *Arbeitsmarktintegration Geflüchteter*, www.ihk-berlin.de/blob/bihk24/politische-positionen-und-statistiken_channel/arbeitsmarkt_beschaeftigung/Download/2957584/eddd5dfade52f15dbe0 73cb596470efc/Broschuere-Arbeitsmarktintegration-von-Asylsuchenden-und-Fluechtlingen-data.pdf.

IHK Berlin (2012), *Der Berliner Arbeitsmarkt vom Sorgenkind zum Hoffnungsträger*, https://www.ihk-berlin.de/blob/bihk24/politische-positionen-und-statistiken_channel/arbeitsmarkt_beschaeftigung/Download/2261282/90b53f509afbc399f911d4ee6fe d27a3/Positionspapier_Der_Berliner_Arbeitsmarkt_Vom_Sorgenkind_zum_Ho-data.pdf.

Integrationsbeauftragte (n.d.). "Die Beauftragte der Bundesregierung für Migration, Flüchtlinge und Integration. Themen. Gesellschaft und Teilhabe. Gesundheit und Integration. Arbeitskreis Migration und Öffentliche Gesundheit", www.integrationsbeauftragte.de/Webs/IB/DE/Themen/GesellschaftUndTeilhabe/Gesundheit/gesundh eit-arbeitskreis.html, (accessed January 2018).

Integrationsgipfel (2014), "Bundesregierung. Teilnehmnerliste", www.bundesregierung.de/Content/DE/Artikel/IB/Artikel/Integrationsgipfel/2014-11-28-anlage-teilnehmerliste.html, (accessed January 2018).

Integrationsgipfel (2015), "Bundesregierung. Teilnehmnerliste", www.bundesregierung.de/Content/DE/Artikel/IB/Artikel/Integrationsgipfel/Integrationsgipfel-2015/2015-11-16-teilnehmerliste.html, (accessed January 2018).

Integrationsmonitoring der Länder; Länderoffene Arbeitsgruppe (2017), *Vierter Bericht zum Integrationsmonitoring der Länder 2013 – 2015*, der Konferent der für Integration zuständigen Ministerinnen und Minister / Senatorinnen und Senatoren der Länder, www.integrationsmonitoring-laender.de/sites/default/files/integrationsbericht_2015_endfassung_online.pdf.

Kahn-Zvorničanin, M., L. Koch, D. Schaffranke (2015), *„und jetzt bin ich Integrationslotsin.“ Evaluation des Landesrahmenprogramms Integrationslotsinnen und Integrationslotsen*, www.berlin.de/lb/intmig/_assets/themen/integrationslots-innen/downloads/evaluationsbericht_landesr ahmenprogramm.pdf.

KGSt ; Kommunale Gemeinschaftsstelle für Verwaltungsmanagement (2017), *Kommunales Integrationsmanagment Nr. 7/17*.

Landesamt für Flüchtlingsangelegenheiten (2017), *Berlin - EASY-Zugangsstatistik*.

Leptien, K. (2014), "Germany's Unitary Federalism", *Dietrich Immigration and Federalism in Europe Federal, State and Local Regulatory Competencies in Austria, Belgium, Germany, Italy, Russia, Spain and Switzerland*, IMIS-Beiträge, Osnabrück, https://www.imis.uni-osnabrueck.de/fileadmin/4_Publikationen/PDFs/imis43.pdf.

Mahning, H. (2004), "The Politics of Minority-Majority Relations: How Immigrant Policies Developed in Paris, Berlin and Zurich", in *Citizenship in European Cities*, Routhledge, New York.

Malorny T., L. Raderschall, J. Werner (2016), "ZukunftsMACHER, Die Berliner, Social Impact -Szene arbeitet an einem besseren Morgen", *Stimmen aus Berlin - Gespräche über die Zukunft der Stadt*, Institut Futur, Berlin, www.diss.fu-berlin.de/docs/servlets/MCRFileNodeServlet/FUDOCS_derivate_000000006636/1602_iF-Schriftenreihe_Zukunft-Berlin-Stimmen_MAZF-ebook.pdf.

OECD (2018), *Working together for local integration of migrants and refugees*, OECD Publishing, Paris. https://doi.org/10.1787/9789264085350-en.

OECD (2017a), *The Need for a Territorial Approach to Migrant Integration: The Role of Local Authorities*, OECD, Paris, www.oecd.org/regional/regional-policy/Migrants-in-cities.pdf.

OECD (2017b), *Finding their Way – Labour Market Integration of Refugees in Germany. International Migration Division*, OECD Publishing, Paris, www.oecd.org/els/mig/Finding-their-Way-Germany.pdf.

OECD (2017c), "Who bears the cost of integrating refugees?", *Migration Policy Debates,* No. 13, OECD, Paris, www.oecd.org/els/mig/migration-policy-debates-13.pdf.

OECD (2017d), International Migration Outlook 2017, OECD Publishing, Paris. http://dx.doi.org/10.1787/migr_outlook-2017-en.

OECD (2016a), *International migration outlook*; OECD Publishing, Paris, http://dx.doi.org/10.1787/1999124x.

OECD (2016b), Making Integration Work: Refugees and others in need of protection, OECD. Publishing, Paris, http://dx.doi.org/10.1787/9789264251236-en

OECD/European Union (2015), Indicators of Immigrant Integration 2015: Settling In, OECD Publishing, Paris. http://dx.doi.org/10.1787/9789264234024-en

OECD (2010), *Reviews of Migrant Education - Closing the Gap for Immigrant Students: Policies, Practice and Performance*, OECD Publishing, Paris, http://dx.doi.org/10.1787/9789264075788-en.

OECD (2007), *Jobs for Immigrants. Volume 1. Labour Market integration in Australia, Denmark, Germany and Sweden.* OECD Publishing. Paris, https://doi.org/10.1787/9789264033603-en.

Parlament Berlin (2014), *Arbeitsbericht der AG Wachsende Stadt*, www.parlament-berlin.de/ados/17/WiFoTech/vorgang/wft17-0141-v.pdf.

Pfeffer-Hoffmann, C. (2016), "Magnet Berlin: Zuwanderung europäischer Fachkäfte", in *Fachkräftesicherung durch Integration zunwandender Fachkräfte aus dem EU-Binnenmakt*, Mensch und Buch Verlag, Berlin.

Piccinni, A. and P. Proietti (forthcoming), "Multi-level governance of humanitarian migrants' reception and integration approach for asylum seekers and refugees: From reception mechanisms to local integration policies", *OECD Working Paper*, OECD Publishing, Paris.

Quartiersmanagment Berlin (2016), "Informationen zum Berliner Quartiersmanagment - Das Programm Soziale Stadt", www.quartiersmanagement-berlin.de/fileadmin/user_upload/SSE_Einlegeblatt_2S_2015_Druck_5_5c.pdf., (accessed January 2018).

Rbb24 (2016), "Mehrere Betreiber wollen die PeWoBe-Heime weiterführen", *rbb24*, www.rbb-online.de/politik/thema/fluechtlinge/berlin/2016/08/flchtlingsheime-pewobe-neue-betreiber-interessiert.html.

Rbb24(2015), "70. Sitzung des Berliner Abgeordnetenhauses", rbb24, https://www.rbb-online.de/imparlament/berlin/2015/08--oktober-2015/70--Sitzung-des-Berliner-Abgeordnetenhauses.html.

Schmid, J., J. I. Mansour (2007), "Wohlfahrtsverbände. Interesse und Dienstleistung", in *Interessenverbände in Deutschland,* Springer VS, Berlin.

Schreiber, V. (2011), *Fraktale Sicherheiten- Eine Kritik an der Kommunalen Kriminalitätsprävention,* Transcript Verlag, Bielefeld, www.researchgate.net/profile/Verena_Schreiber2/publication/264547386_Fraktale_Sicherheiten_Eine_Kritik_der_kommunalen_Kriminalpravention/links/53e48aaf0cf21cc29fc90a16/Fraktale-Sicherheiten-Eine-Kritik-der-kommunalen-Kriminalpraevention.pdf.

Stadt Berlin (n.d.), "Senatverwaltung fuer Stadtentwicklung und Wohnen. BENN – Berlin Entwickelt Neue Nachabrschaften Programme", www.stadtentwicklung.berlin.de/staedtebau/foerderprogramme/benn/de/programm.shtml, (accessed January 2018).

Stuttgart (n.d.), "Kommunaler Qualitaetszirkel zur Inetgrationpolitik", www.stuttgart.de/item/show/385012#headline5a69a9ecca4d3, (accessed January 2018).

Sueddeutsche.de Feb 27, 2016 *Berlin wächst - und die Stadt kommt nicht hinterher* http://www.sueddeutsche.de/leben/stadtentwicklung-berlin-waechst-und-die-stadt-kommt-nicht-hinterher-1.2882645 ; see also: Senatskanzlei Berlin (Dec 2014)

SVR; Sachverständigenrat deutscher Stiftungen für Integration und Migration (2014), *Forschungsbereich; Diskriminierung am Ausbildungsmarkt - Ausmaß, Ursachen und Handlungsperspektiven*, www.bosch-stiftung.de/sites/default/files/publications/pdf_import/SVR-FB_Diskriminierung-am-Ausbildungsmarkt.pdf.

Tagesspiegel (2015). Fluechtline for dem Lageso in Berlin. Schlage stehen bei 38 Grad. *Tagesspiegel*, https://www.tagesspiegel.de/berlin/fluechtlinge-vor-dem-lageso-in-berlin-schlange-stehen-bei-38-grad/12162194.html.

UNSD (2017), "International migration statistics", United Nations Statistics Division, https://unstats.un.org/unsd/demographic/sconcerns/migration/migrmethods.htm#B.

Further Reading

Eisnecker, Philipp; Schupp, Jürgen (2016) Stimmungsbarometer zu Geflüchteten in Deutschland: Stabil hohes Engagement in der Gesellschaft für Geflüchtete bei weiterhin überwiegend negativer Einschätzung der Auswirkungen der Flüchtlingszuwanderung. SOEPpapers DIW Berlin

Federal Office for Migration and Refugees (2013), Die Organisation der Aufnahme und Unterbringung von Asylbewerbern in Deutschland. German National Contact Point for the European Migration Network (EMN), Working Paper

Gesemann, F. (2016) Kommunale Integrationspolitik. Springer Fachmedien Wiesbaden 2016. H.U. Brinkmann und M. Sauer (Editor), Einwanderungsgesellschaft Deutschland, DOI 10.1007/978-3-658-05746-6_11

Gesemann, Frank Dr. / Roth, Roland Prof. Dr. (2012) Stand der kommunalen Integrationspolitik in Deutschland. Study Institut für Demokratische Entwicklung und Soziale Integration (DESI) ExWoSt-Forschungsfeldes „Integration und Stadtteilpolitik" des Bundesministeriums für Verkehr Bau und Stadtentwicklung, betreut durch das Bundesinsitut für Bau-, Stadt und Raumforschung

SVR – Sachverständigenrat deutscher Stiftungen für Integration und Migration (2013) Erfolgsfall Europa? Folgen und Herausforderungen der EU-Freizügigkeit für Deutschland Jahresgutachten 2013 mit Migrationsbarometer.

Thähnhardt, Dietrich (2013) Migrantenorganisationen, Engagement, Transnationalität und Integration. Expertise und Dokumentation zur Wirtschaftspolitik, Gesprächskreis Migration und Integration, Friedrich-Ebert-Stiftung.

Annex A. List of participants in the interviews with OECD delegation 8 and 9 March 2017

Federal Chancellery of Germany

- Honey Deiheimi, Head of Division – Social Integration at the office of the Federal Commissioner for Migration, Refugees and Integration.
- Marius Dietrich, Head of Unit - Social Integration at the office of the Federal Commissioner for Migration, Refugees and Integration.

Federal Ministry of Federal Ministry for Economic Affairs and Energy (BMWi)

- Mr. Till Spannagel, Division EA3 - Co-ordination of EU Cohesion and Structural Policy

Senate of Berlin

- Andreas Germershausen, Commissioner of Integration of the Berlin Senate.
- Robin Schneider, Head of Section for Central Integration Affairs,
- Nele Allenberg, Head of Section Welcome Center Berlin
- Imke Juretzka, Policy advisor refugee policy
- Doris Nahawandi, Policy advisor Muslim life and antidiscrimination
- Kai Leptien, Policy advisor integration monitoring and 'Integrationslotsen'

Council District Berlin Mitte

- Noemi Majer, refugee coordinator,
- Ronald Schäfer, Head of Citizen office, Berlin Mitte
- Gisela Schön, Head of project „Die Brücke", Citizen office, Berlin Mitte

NGOs

- Orkan Özdemir, Managing director, Berlin needs you!
- Ms. Hafener, Managing director, Diakonisches Werk Steglitz und Teltow-Zehlendorf e.V. (DWSTZ)
- Ms. Hamzagic, head of unit, Diakonisches Werk Steglitz und Teltow-Zehlendorf e.V. (DWSTZ)
- Gökcen Demiragli, Director of integration and refugee support at Nachbarschaftsheim Schöneberg
- Jessica Mettlen, Managing director, Refugee Schelter Rathaus Friedenau
- Joachim Rüffer, Managing Director, KommMit e.V.

- Alexander Fourestié, Project coordinator, Kiezküchen Gmbh
- Regina Schmid-Rossleben, Project coordinator, Bildungsmarkt, e.V

UNHCR Berlin

- Norbert Trosien, Associate Protection Officer
- Julia Moser, Protection Associate

Annex B. Overview of integration concepts and regulations at national and city level

Berlin has a long-standing history of integration policy making. The first Commissioner for Foreigners and a cross-sectorial working unit was established as early as in 1981. The position and unit were set up in response to large numbers of family reunifications of so called "guest-workers". The main aim in establishing this new position was to combat discrimination and provide social and emergency counselling for newcomers in the city. Public campaigning to communicate the added value to the citizens of Berlin was part of the tasks of the units and commissioners. They also established a platform to network the many different volunteer and social initiatives in the city. Berlin was the first among the Länder to introduce a position as such in the federal republic. In 2003, a new person took over the post, which was subsequently renamed the "Commissioner for Migration and Integration". In 2005, Berlin introduced its first integration concept, which was revised in 2007 and finally led to the establishment of the Participation and Integration Law. The latter guides today's integration principles of the Berlin Commissioner for Migration and Integration.

At the federal level, the lack of a federal integration policy underwent a paradigm shift in early 2000. Inequities affecting the migrant population in Germany had become particularly visible in the field of education, political participation and employment (Federal Office for Migration and Refugees, 2005: 46). Shortcomings in educational policy were also revealed by the poor performance of German students in the first INES/OECD Programme for International Student Assessment report (PISA) in 2001 (Berlin Senate, 2005). This stirred debate in Germany, and came to be known as the "PISA shock", which centred on the fact that students' educational attainment is largely dependent on the origin and educational achievement of their parents. In 2004 the first Integration Summit (Integrationsgipfel) took place brought the issue to the national stage. The longstanding experiences of municipalities and third sector actors were included in this process. The federal chancellor, churches, religious communities, welfare umbrella organisations, *Länder* and municipal and migrant representatives took part. As an outcome of the summit the National Integration Plan was formulated (*Nationaler Integrations Plan*) and implemented in 2007. It is the first document that summarises a national integration mission and aims to approach past shortcomings in integration by improving language training and education, encouraging dialogue with migrant communities and other actors and especially safeguarding the rights of migrant women and girls. Subsequently, the National Integration Plan was revised and the National Action Plan was introduced (last revision 2012). The comprehensive framework includes the areas of education, labour market, sports, arts, media, as well as regional integration. The German integration strategy also perceives EU-migrants as a target group in the action plan. It defines targets, responsibilities, and is to be evaluated on a regular basis. Also, integration measures were included in federal law for the first time in 2005 (first Integration law).

Annex C. Distribution of Competencies Across Levels of Government

Policy Area	National Government	Länder/state level	District level
Multiple Areas, specifically targeting Asylum seekers and refugees	Initial reception and allocation Asylum application assessment and status recognition (BAMF) Refugees/After recognition: Social welfare and healthcare for all refugees, who have a legal residence card. Integration courses for recognised refugees and asylum seekers with an above-average recognition rate (>50%). At the time of writing people originating from Syria, Eritrea, Iraq, Iran and Somalia. (100 educational units: 60 units of German classes, 40 units on cultural background). Regulation and measures for access to the labour market for asylum seekers and refugees Early integration opportunities (FIM)	Provision of Accommodation in reception centres, emergency accommodation and/or joint accommodation (LAF) Provision of allowance during asylum claim assessment (LAF) Provide early integration/language courses for all other asylum seekers, who are not eligible to take part in the federal language course. Early integration opportunities such as studying, work or volunteer opportunities (e.g. ARRIVO, bridge, Welcome Centre, etc.,)	Volunteer activities and neighbourhood projects to support integration and reception
Education	Research and Project Funding, including German Federal Training Assistance (BaFög), Together with state level and companies it regulates the German Vocational Training System.	Design of the education system Provision of financial means for teachers and for maintenance of schools Orientation, guidelines and general curriculum for schools	Maintenance of primary and secondary education, provision of school places Schools: Supervision / implementation and design of lessons and composition of classes (including welcome classes) Assessment and placement of newcomers Provide courses for asylum seekers and refugees who are not eligible for federal language courses
Language learning	Federal integration courses for language training are implemented by the BAMF (subordinated to the BMI), which contracts private and public entities on the local level.		
Vocational training policy	Federal Employment Agency (BMAS) funds and initiates projects across the country.		
Social Policy	The German government sets the criteria for social welfare allocation. The Federal Employment agency subordinated body (Agentur für Arbeit) has regional sub offices.	Elderly and child care Social integration of people with disabilities	Social assistance: social welfare, welfare payments, social services administration (Jobcenter and Social Welfare Offices)

Employment	The German government (BMAS) sets the criteria for social welfare (unemployment benefits) and regulations for access to the labour market. The Federal Employment agency subordinated body (Agentur für Arbeit) has regional sub offices, which initiates activating measures.	Social integration of foreigners Youth policy: financing youth organisations; youth and child protection; youth probation and youth care. Youth assistance and welfare services	
Housing	Provides grants for building social housing Social Housing policy (Wohnungs- berechtigungsschein)	Construction of (Social) Housing	
Spatial Planning		Urban and Spatial Planning (Senate Department for Urban Development and Housing)	
Public Health	No federal health policy for asylum seekers, refugees and undocumented migrants in place Federal German Social Welfare includes statutory health insurance for everyone with a valid residence permit Regulations for protection of vulnerable categories	Healthcare for asylum seekers and rejected asylum seekers (Health Card) Assessment of vulnerability and implementing of federal standards	
Public Administration	Naturalisation Test and granting of naturalisation	Encouraging Intercultural Openness of Public Institutions (Commissioner for Migration and Integration) Issue of residence and work permits and repatriations (Immigration Authorities)	Registration of Citizens Administration of Naturalisations (Application process)
Public order and Safety	Authority in all matters regarding immigration Federal security framework	Maintenance of security on the local level (Police, Fire Brigade) Local Security Framework	
Economic development	Federal economic policy	Local economic policy	

Source: Findings from OECD visit (8-9 March 2017); Berlin Municipality (2017).

Annex D. Statistics on Asylum Applications in Germany

According to BAMF (2016), in 2015 Germany acknowledged an increase in asylum applications in comparison to 2014 by 155.3% (441 899 applications) and made decisions on 282 726 asylum applications, of which 49.8% were positive decisions (140 915 positive decisions). The majority of applications were submitted by Syrians (35.9%), followed by Albanians (12.2%) and Kosovars (7.6%). Albanian and Kosovar requests have a very low rate of asylum recognition (Albania: 0.2%; Kosovo: 0.4%), whereas Syrian (96% of applicants were recognised as refugees in 2015) Iraqi (88.6% in 2015) and Afghans (47.6% in 2015) have a higher rate. In 2016 the number of applicants further increased sharply (63.5% increase compared to 2015). The BAMF received 722 370 first applications for asylum, of which 62.4% were granted (433 920 positive decisions). According BAMF (2016), Most applications were made (36.9 %) for Syrians (recognition rate 98%), followed by 17.6% for Afghans (recognition rate 55.8%) and 13.3% for Iraqis (recognition rate 70.2%). The sharp increase in 2016 does not reflect a high inflow but rather a backlog in the handling of applications submitted in 2015 (OECD, 2016:190/191).

ORGANISATION FOR ECONOMIC CO-OPERATION AND DEVELOPMENT

The OECD is a unique forum where governments work together to address the economic, social and environmental challenges of globalisation. The OECD is also at the forefront of efforts to understand and to help governments respond to new developments and concerns, such as corporate governance, the information economy and the challenges of an ageing population. The Organisation provides a setting where governments can compare policy experiences, seek answers to common problems, identify good practice and work to co-ordinate domestic and international policies.

The OECD member countries are: Australia, Austria, Belgium, Canada, Chile, the Czech Republic, Denmark, Estonia, Finland, France, Germany, Greece, Hungary, Iceland, Ireland, Israel, Italy, Japan, Korea, Latvia, Lithuania, Luxembourg, Mexico, the Netherlands, New Zealand, Norway, Poland, Portugal, the Slovak Republic, Slovenia, Spain, Sweden, Switzerland, Turkey, the United Kingdom and the United States. The European Union takes part in the work of the OECD.

OECD Publishing disseminates widely the results of the Organisation's statistics gathering and research on economic, social and environmental issues, as well as the conventions, guidelines and standards agreed by its members.

OECD PUBLISHING, 2, rue André-Pascal, 75775 PARIS CEDEX 16
(85 2018 18 1 P) ISBN 978-92-64-30522-9 – 2018

www.ingramcontent.com/pod-product-compliance
Lightning Source LLC
Chambersburg PA
CBHW081844250726

48659CB00008B/2610